Keeping Children Safe

Introduction

1. In the last few years, there have been several severe cases of child abuse resulting in the death of a child, including Lauren Wright and Victoria Climbié. However, these children were not the first to die at the hands of their carers. There has been a series of high profile deaths over the last 30 years, such as Kimberley Carlile, Jasmine Beckford, and Tyra Henry in the 1980s, which together influenced the development of the Children Act 1989.

2. After Victoria Climbié's death, the Government set up a statutory inquiry into the events surrounding her killing, in order to find out whether or not it was time to look again at the statutory framework for child protection in this country. Lord Laming's report was published on 28th January 2003.

3. In addition, in response to the commitment in the 1998 White Paper *Modernising Social Services*, eight inspectorates have carried out joint inspections of children's safeguards, with the Joint Chief Inspectors publishing their report, *Safeguarding Children*, in October 2002.

4. These reports show a number of problems with the current system for safeguarding children. But they also show us how to move towards a better children's safeguards system, where child protection services are not separate from support for families, but are part of the spectrum of services provided to help and support children and families.

5. Safeguarding is taken to mean:

- All agencies working with children, young people and their families take all reasonable measures to ensure that the risks of harm to children's welfare are minimised; and

- Where there are concerns about children and young people's welfare, all agencies take all appropriate actions to address those concerns, working to agreed local policies and procedures in full partnership with other local agencies.

6. This document sets out the Government's response to both reports, and covers:

- What is wrong with the system now (paragraphs 7-9);

- What needs to be in a children's safeguards system for the 21st century (paragraphs 10-13);

- What the Government is doing, covering:

    - Prevention and early intervention (paragraphs 15-17);

- Improving working together across agencies and organisations (paragraphs 18-39);
- Assuring good practice in social services, the NHS and police (paragraphs 40-47);
- Rationalising Government guidance (paragraphs 48-57);
- Bringing information together (paragraphs 58-77);
- Workforce issues (paragraphs 78-90);
- Other issues (public protection issues, private fostering, the services that failed Victoria) (paragraphs 91-100);
- How the Government will know the system is improving (paragraphs 101-116);
- Learning lessons from experience (paragraphs 117-121); and
- Conclusion.

What is wrong with the system now?

7. The reports show that the legislative framework for safeguarding children set out in the Children Act 1989 is basically sound. However, there are serious weaknesses in the way in which it is interpreted, resourced and implemented.

8. The Victoria Climbié Inquiry Report showed that the system failed comprehensively, because of ill-trained and overworked staff, who were unsupported by their managers or more senior staff in their organisations, and because of senior staff failing to take responsibility for the quality of children's services in the organisation. *Safeguarding Children* showed that, although Victoria's was an extreme case, there were issues emerging from it that are also relevant elsewhere.

9. Particular problems include:

- Organisations (and therefore their staff) give different levels of priority to the safeguarding of children, and work to different standards. This makes it difficult for professionals to work together effectively;

- Leading on from this, Area Child Protection Committees are often weak, with no authority and few resources to carry out their functions. In addition, they often suffer from lack of senior representation from organisations other than social services;

- In practice, the system does not always focus on the child's needs. For example, in Victoria's case, the focus was on the needs of the adults responsible for her, rather than the child herself;

- Senior managers, right up to Chief Executives and Chairmen, do not know enough about, and take enough responsibility for, the actions of their staff;

- Social services staff may make decisions about whether or not to assess a child's needs (and if there is no assessment, the child will not receive any services) based on whether the child appears to be 'in need' or a 'child protection' case. However, since it is rarely clear without an assessment whether or not a child is in fact being harmed, this causes two main problems: firstly, children and families do not get services early enough to prevent harm, and secondly, staff in other organisations describe all referrals as 'child protection' in a well-meaning attempt to ensure that the children concerned get support;

- Many of the organisations working with children and families have difficulties recruiting and retaining skilled and qualified staff;

- Many staff are not adequately trained in safeguarding children. This is a particular problem for staff who come into contact with children and families on a regular basis, but are not considered to be 'child protection specialists';

- There are some fundamental deficiencies in basic professional practice, often made worse by poor managerial practice;

- In many areas, there is too much local guidance, which is often out of date, and does not necessarily provide practitioners with the information they need;

- Many staff do not know when to share information about a child and family, and what information can and should be shared under what circumstances;

- Children in custody are not adequately safeguarded; and

- Multi-Agency Public Protection Arrangements, although in very early stages of development, have already begun to develop very different practice across the country.

A children's safeguards system for the 21st century

10. In order to safeguard children, everyone working with children and families must provide services that reduce the risks of children being harmed. In addition, if they have concerns about a specific child, they must take action to protect that child from harm, working in partnership with all other relevant organisations.

11. An effective system to safeguard children should have: *link in with baby P case*

- A sound statutory framework, which balances the interests of children, parents and the State, and allows practitioners to respond quickly and effectively to concerns about a child;

- People from different organisations and professional backgrounds working together effectively, supported by a full commitment to safeguarding children from each of their organisations;

- Thorough and co-ordinated assessments of the child's needs, including the need for protection, and the parents' or carers' ability to meet those needs; *did this happen?*

- A range of services, provided by different organisations and community groups to meet the assessed needs of children and families;

- Where services are provided for adults who are parents, staff who consider the impact that these services (or the parent's need for the services) will have on the children;

- Children and family members involved in making decisions about what services they receive; *does this...*

- A focus on achieving better outcomes for children; *? ECM + children in care happen?*

- Information about whether the system is effective, both for individual children, and for the whole population, including through inspection of services;

- Adequate numbers of staff;

- Adequate training for all staff working with children and families, including through continuous professional development; and

- Good supervision of staff working with children and families, including monitoring of individual cases.

12. An effective system for safeguarding children, therefore, has staff from one or more organisations working together to support families before there are specific concerns about a child's safety, with continuing assessment and review to seek improvements to the system. By ensuring universal services, such as health and education, are accessible to all children and families, and targeted services, such as Sure Start and additional support in school for children with special educational needs, are provided to reduce the stress on particular children and families, the risk of possible harm to children is reduced.

what about child P ?

13. Abuse and neglect of children will inevitably remain a substantial problem, with children dying at the hands of their parents or carers, albeit in very small numbers, an unavoidable feature. The children's services system must therefore be able to protect and support those children who are at risk of abuse or neglect. Although the Government does not believe that child deaths can be eliminated entirely, action is still needed – by supporting families more effectively, and at an earlier stage, the extent and seriousness of abuse and neglect can and will be lowered.

Early Prevention needed

What will the Government do to improve things?

14. The challenge in improving children's services is to ensure that any necessary changes are made, and also that Government policy and the law are correctly and consistently applied in all areas and by all those involved in safeguarding children's welfare. Alongside this document, the Government has published a Green Paper *Every Child Matters* setting out a vision for reforming and strengthening services for children, young people and their families.

(2003)

Prevention and early intervention

15. The Green Paper chapters *Strong Foundations* and *Supporting Families and Carers* set out how the Government will improve support for parents and families. They explain what will be done to make family support services more accessible, through a wider range of universal services, provided without stigma, and easy to access, targeted services for specific groups, and specialist support for individual children and families. *explain – every case is different*

16. The Green Paper also sets out what is being done to support children and families who are affected by problems that are often linked to poor outcomes for children, such as domestic violence, drug and alcohol misuse, mental health problems, and learning disabilities, to build on what the Government has already done, such as the establishment of Sure Start, the Children's Fund, and Connexions. For example, the Government has just launched a new strategy on domestic violence, and will continue to tackle the eradication of child poverty as a priority.

17. The chapter *Strong Foundations* sets out the Government's existing plans for, and the Green Paper consults on improvements to, more specialist services. For example, Child and Adolescent Mental Health Services are already being expanded, with all areas planned to be delivering a comprehensive service by 2006. The Government is consulting on standards for temporary accommodation for homeless families and proposals to produce clear guidance on the arrangements that should be put in place to ensure that all households placed in temporary accommodation by housing authorities receive support to ensure their health, education and social care needs are met.

Improving working together

Making safeguarding children a priority

18. It was clear from both reports that professionals find it hard to work together effectively because of the different levels of priority given by their organisations to safeguarding children.

19. The Green Paper chapter *Accountability and Integration – Locally, Regionally and Nationally* sets out proposals to improve the co-ordination of services at national and local level. On 13th June 2003, the Prime Minister announced the appointment of Margaret Hodge as Minister for Children, Young People and Families bringing together the responsibility for children's education and social services into one Government Department, and providing a strong focus for children's policy at the national level. Locally, the Government will encourage the development of Children's Trusts, which will work with other organisations in the area. Subject to consultation, Local Safeguarding Children Boards will be created as the statutory successors to Area Child Protection Committees.

20. The Green Paper chapter *Early Intervention and Effective Protection* explains how front line workers will be better able to work together, backed by innovative solutions to information sharing, such as those being developed by the trailblazers for the Identification, Referral and Tracking project, and unified assessments. This should help them to make better decisions, and draw resources together more effectively. This will be supported by joint line management and supervision, the pooling of resources and improved commissioning arrangements.

21. In addition, the Green Paper stresses that the Government will raise the priority given to safeguarding children in relevant organisations, and ensure that their objectives and priorities are more consistent. As a first step towards this, on publication of the Victoria Climbié Inquiry Report on 28th January 2003, the then Secretary of State for Health wrote to all NHS bodies and councils with social services responsibilities to remind them of their responsibilities towards children, including the fact that the provision of adequate child protection services is a statutory responsibility for councils, and that these responsibilities should be reflected when setting budgets and managing performance.

22. The National Policing Plan, published in November 2002, set out the Government's priorities for the police. For the first time, child protection was specifically included in these priorities, although not within the four key priorities. This placing has been criticised, and the Home Office will review this before the next National Policing Plan is published.

23. Local policing plans were submitted to the Home Office at the end of March 2003. The Home Office is satisfied that all the local policing plans contain appropriate strategies for safeguarding children and are consistent with the National Policing Plan.

24. At the same time, a police working group has been looking at the issue of whether or not child protection teams should be staffed, in whole or in part, by trained detectives. The group suggested that, ideally, child protection teams should be entirely staffed by CID-trained officers, but recognised that there needed to be some flexibility in view of the fact that not all the work of child protection teams is about serious crime. However, the Association of Chief Police Officers has now decided that all child protection officers should be trained to detective standard by the end of 2005.

25. The Government has also taken further action in other areas to raise the priority of safeguarding children:

- Child protection has been an explicit high priority for the Probation Service for many years. In the new assessment system for offenders (OASys), assessment of the risk of harm to children is an explicit part of the process for all offenders supervised by the probation service. The protection of children also featured as a national priority in the recently published National Prioritisation Framework. This identified key areas of work, to be delivered even in the event of reduced resource being available. Local area plans will take account of this requirement;

- The establishment of the new Public Protection Unit in the National Probation Directorate in the Home Office is a reflection of the importance attached to the issue of protecting the public from harm, and child protection is an explicit part of the Unit's remit;

- The Department for Education and Skills is making it a statutory requirement that Local Education Authorities, and the governing bodies of both schools and further education institutions make arrangements to carry out their functions with a view to safeguarding and promoting the welfare of children, and have regard to guidance issued by the Secretary of State in drawing up those arrangements. The new duty under the Education Act 2002 will come into force on 1st April 2004. The Department for Education and Skills will issue new guidance, and use a network of centrally funded regional co-ordinators, to help authorities and governing bodies meet the new requirement in regard to child protection. A similar requirement will apply to independent schools from 1st September 2003;

- The Department for Education and Skills is also introducing a requirement for Local Education Authorities to have a Single Education Plan, to rationalise the planning of education services and ensure an explicit commitment to safeguarding and promoting child welfare. These plans will be introduced in 10 local authorities in 2004, and in all local authorities by 2006;

- From 1st April 2001, all Children and Family Court Advisory and Support Service Regions in England and Wales have been represented on Area Child Protection Committees. This reflects the priority given to safeguarding children in service delivery, training and the role of staff in safeguarding children in Family Court Proceedings;

- Chief executives of upper-tier and unitary authorities were asked in September 2002 to ensure that, from April 2003, there is a Local Preventative Strategy in place for their area. While these strategies will have a much broader scope than child protection, the principles to guide their development contain explicit reference to "responding to the need for local agencies to work together to safeguard children and promote their well-being";

- Jacqui Smith, the then Minister of State for Health, wrote to all Primary Care Trust (PCT) chief executives on 28th January 2002, setting out their responsibilities for safeguarding children, and particularly the need to appoint a PCT Director to take responsibility for child protection, and designated child protection professionals to provide advice on child protection to other professionals in the area;

- The Department of Health has published guidelines for general practitioners (GPs) with special interests, including one set for GPs with a special interest in child protection, developed with the Royal College of General Practitioners. These guidelines draw on existing good practice, to advise GPs with the appropriate skills and experience about providing a specialist child protection service in primary care. The core activities of a GP with a special interest in child protection will be to improve the understanding and capability of other practitioners to respond to suspected or actual cases of abuse or neglect, working closely with other child protection specialists and organisations in order to do so.

Common standards

26. The Green Paper chapter *Accountability and Integration – Locally, Regionally and Nationally* sets out how, to support local integration, the Government will rationalise performance targets, plans and indicators and will set out practice standards expected of each agency in relation to children.

27. So that all health and social services bodies work to common standards, the Government published the first part of the National Service Framework for Children, Young People and Maternity Services, including a standard for hospital services, on 10th April 2003. The full Framework, to be published in 2004, will set standards covering child protection services, against which health and social care organisations will be inspected. The National Service Framework is a ten year programme for improving health and social care services for children and young people.

28. The hospital standard takes account of those recommendations in the Victoria Climbié Inquiry Report which apply to children in hospital. It sets out aspirations for a service that is child-centred, and offers high quality services, provided by appropriately trained staff, in a suitable environment that recognises the particular needs of children and young people, at different stages of their lives.

29. Issues addressed in the hospital standard in response to the concerns in the Victoria Climbié Inquiry Report include:

- Changing cultural attitudes, so that staff consider whether a child's injury or illness might be a result of abuse or neglect;

- Having interpreting services that support staff in recognising the particular needs of a child who may be at risk of harm;

- Reinforcing the duty of the local authority to safeguard and promote the welfare of children in their area, including those who are in hospital, by actions such as taking responsibility for the child's safety and welfare whilst they are in hospital and working with other local authorities and agencies to provide services for the child or family;

- Agreeing and recording a multi-agency action plan before the child leaves hospital and emphasising that the need to safeguard a child should always inform the timing of discharge from hospital;

- Having records of hospital care which are contemporaneous, clear, accurate, comprehensive, attributable to and signed by the health care professional providing the service and the responsible consultant where appropriate, and which detail any prior attendance at that hospital or another;

- Having clinical governance systems in hospitals that reflect the particular needs of children, which should be reinforced by appointing a board level children's lead within the trust. The board should be informed about the trust's performance in relation to child protection; and

- Adequate support and supervision for staff in their safeguarding role.

30. Safeguarding children has been identified as one of the main themes running through the whole of the National Service Framework. Both the hospital standard and the Emerging Findings document, published alongside, included a draft standard on safeguarding children, for consultation. This is likely to be included in the main Framework when it is published, which will also set out what organisations should do to meet the standard and illustrate different ways of doing so.

Clinical governance and quality of care

31. One of Lord Laming's recommendations was that child protection should be brought within the framework of clinical governance. Child protection and the systems in place for identifying and managing child abuse and neglect, and safeguarding children, already form an integral part of clinical governance. The National Service Framework hospital standard made this unambiguous and illustrated how clinical governance systems should recognise the needs of children and young people as a specific group. NHS staff, as well as patients and carers, will be able to report any incidents that have, or might have, affected the safety of a child in hospital to the National Patient Safety Agency. The Agency will not investigate individual cases, but will use this information to identify patterns and trends of incidents at a national level and to develop practical solutions to prevent them being repeated.

32. In addition, the Clinical Governance Support Team in the NHS Modernisation Agency has provided, and will continue to provide, support in the development of policy and practice regarding clinical governance in children's services.

33. These developments are only a few of those being taken to improve clinical quality. The NHS Plan and the Department of Health's response to Sir Ian Kennedy's report of the public inquiry into children's heart surgery at the Bristol Royal Infirmary detail a number of initiatives designed to improve the regulation, education and training of health care professionals, including continuous professional development, joint training modules, appraisal and revalidation.

Organisational culture

34. Lord Laming found that, in Victoria's case, once a senior doctor had appeared to rule out child protection concerns, other healthcare staff, social workers and police had found it difficult to question that decision. This is unlikely to be an isolated occurrence. Therefore, the Department of Health asked the Royal College of Paediatrics and Child Health to identify options for addressing differences of opinion between healthcare staff, and between healthcare and other staff, especially in relation to child protection concerns.

35. The Royal College held a workshop, which identified a number of issues to be covered in Government guidance, including minimum standards for organisations working on safeguarding children, covering areas such as releasing staff for training, continuous professional development, and supervision, and systems for regular audit of child protection cases.

36. The workshop also made recommendations around training, which will inform the review of inter-agency training on safeguarding children currently in progress, and the two sets of training materials being prepared, one by the Royal College with support from Government, and one separately commissioned by the Government to support the implementation of guidance.

Breaking down barriers

37. The Green Paper chapter *Accountability and Integration – Locally, Regionally and Nationally* explains how key services will be better integrated. As a first stage in this, the Government has announced 35 Children's Trusts pathfinders which will develop the integration of education, health and social services for children, as well as other services such as Connexions and Youth Offending Teams.

38. Children's Trusts will be working towards a single planning and commissioning function supported by pooled budgets. The pathfinders may start from a more focused position, and may concentrate on integrating provision initially, but there is a clear anticipation that they will pull together all the strands of services for children, which will be important in achieving a coherent approach towards child protection.

39. Key requirements of the Children's Trust pathfinders include having clear governance and accountability arrangements for the partnership to lead, manage and monitor the work of the Trust. The Director of Children's Services will take responsibility for the services in the Children's Trust. Trusts are also required to have a clear, agreed plan and objectives, that fit in with local strategic planning. The work of the Trust must be supported by a written agreement, setting out the way in which the Trust is going to work, the level of resources, and how those resources are going to be deployed. It is important that these fundamental building blocks of partnership are put in place to secure clarity of intent and activity, including that for child protection.

Assuring basic good practice

40. It was clear from Lord Laming's report that poor professional practice was a major problem.

41. Therefore, when his report was published, Government ministers sent a checklist of all the recommendations that are about basic good professional practice to chief executives of all NHS bodies and councils with social services responsibilities, and Chief Constables of all police forces. They were asked to guarantee, within three months, that this basic good practice was in place. This checklist was followed up with a self-audit tool from the Social Services Inspectorate for councils, and the Commission for Health Improvement for NHS bodies, to assist senior managers and elected members in assessing whether or not their organisations are meeting all the necessary standards. The Association of Chief Police Officers followed up the checklist with a letter to all forces, asking them about their practice.

42. The responses to these audit tools and checklist, once fully analysed, will give a picture of the priority given to child protection across the NHS, social services and the police. The three inspectorates have received a full response rate and feedback has indicated that the field has found the audit exercise useful in reinforcing good practice and in identifying areas for development. The initial findings from the audit tools are:

Commission for Health Improvement

- There is a lack of clarity about strategic health authorities' and primary care trusts' responsibilities for performance management in child protection;

- Not all of the organisations' Boards demonstrate sufficient awareness of or responsibility for child protection issues;

- Cross-agency and cross-boundary working are very variable;

- Not all organisations have named nurses, doctors and midwives (where relevant) for child protection.

Her Majesty's Inspectorate of Constabulary

- Whilst all police forces are working to improve the supervision of cases, and this will be monitored by Her Majesty's Inspectorate of Constabulary, a number of forces indicated that they currently have insufficient capacity to meet some of the recommendations;

- The audit indicates that there has been a tendency for forces to focus solely upon the operation of their child protection units rather than considering the wider implications for the force as a whole; and

- The responsibility for reporting initial concerns to the police clearly rests with social services, and police forces are working with councils to seek to ensure notification of potential crimes at the earliest opportunity, in accordance with Government guidance. This will need to be supported by rigorous recording and auditing on the part of the police and such arrangements do not yet appear to be in place across the service.

Social Services Inspectorate

- More than half of the councils have been evaluated by the Social Services Inspectorate as serving children well or serving most children well, with excellent or promising capacity for improvement with a further quarter having promising capacity for improvement;

- The better performing councils have policies and procedures in place, and also have systems for ensuring that the policies and procedures are put into practice; and

- In just less than a quarter of councils, there was some level of unallocated child protection cases, and a number of councils were experiencing significant recruitment problems.

43. Once the full findings of the self-audits and police checklist have been analysed and reported, the Government will decide, based on the findings, what further action needs to be taken to ensure that all organisations give a high enough priority to safeguarding children.

44. The Social Services Inspectorate has followed up concerns about specific councils through its annual review process. Inspections of children's services had taken place or were already planned in all councils where the audit raised particular concerns.

45. The Commission for Health Improvement will develop self-assessment tools for clinicians and inspection methods in order to carry out follow-up inspections of children's safeguards in the NHS. The inspection timetable will be influenced by the establishment of the Commission for Health Audit and Inspection.

46. Her Majesty's Inspectorate of Constabulary is providing individual feedback to all forces in relation to their implementation of the recommendations and the overview of progress across the service provided by the audit. Those forces which appear to be unlikely to meet the relevant recommendations within three or six months will continue to be monitored within the inspection programme, so as to ensure that progress is maintained, and services improved accordingly.

47. The findings of these audits and inspections will influence the further development of the National Service Framework for children.

Government guidance

48. Lord Laming found that there was too much, and outdated, local guidance, which did not tell practitioners what to do in order to safeguard children. Therefore, the then Secretary of State for Health announced that the Government would issue shorter, clearer guidance to all those involved in safeguarding children and revise the Children Act 1989 guidance to shorten it and bring it fully up to date. The revised guidance would also address the Joint Chief Inspectors' concern that councils were at risk of only assessing those children who were already considered to be in need of protection and not those where more general concerns had been expressed.

What To Do If You're Worried A Child Is Being Abused

49. On 19th May 2003, six Government Departments issued a booklet called *What To Do If You're Worried A Child Is Being Abused*, which communicates directly with people working with children and families, and explains their role in the safeguarding process. This role is set out in existing Government guidance *Working Together to Safeguard Children* and the *Framework for the Assessment of Children in Need and their Families*. The booklet is designed to help people to protect children more effectively, through a better understanding of what to do about any concerns, and particularly, when to refer them to social services.

50. Child protection is everyone's responsibility: both staff who come into direct contact with children, and those who work with adults who are parents and/or carers. Chief executives were therefore asked to pass the summary of the booklet to everyone who comes into contact with children, parents or families as part of their work.

51. The booklet makes clear that children's needs should be assessed, and services provided to meet those needs, including the need for protection, regardless of whether or not they are reported, at the point of referral, to be 'children in need' or 'child protection' referrals.

52. The booklet also contains a short section on sharing information. This takes a new approach to information sharing, as it steers people through the process of deciding whether to share information, and if so, what to share, with whom and why. It explains, in a clear and concise way, the issues involved in making decisions about sharing information. It also provides people with the necessary references to locate more detailed guidance should they need further assistance. This section of the booklet was written with the help of the General Medical Council.

Further guidance

53. The revised Children's Services Guidance will consist of two core documents, one for people working directly with children and families, and their managers, and one for organisations. These two documents will bring together information from previous publications, and set out the processes for assessment, planning, intervention and review of all children who come into contact with social services, and the responsibilities of organisations to put in place systems that enable children to be safeguarded effectively, including for proper supervision and training of staff.

54. The Green Paper proposes a common core assessment, building on existing frameworks, including the *Framework for the Assessment of Children in Need and their Families*. The categories from that framework – children's developmental needs, parenting capacity and family and environmental factors – will provide the 'common language' and approach for everyone to use to help them to identify children about whom they are concerned, why they are concerned, who is best placed to respond to those concerns and what outcome is being sought from any planned response.

55. The core guidance to organisations will cover the following issues:

- The priority given to children's services, and within that to safeguarding children;

- The roles and responsibilities of all agencies and organisations in relation to the provision of services to children in need generally, and also for the safeguarding of children;

- How people should work together, including issues such as making arrangements for safe discharge from hospital for a child;

- Ensuring that staff are competent, including making checks when recruiting staff and training (including induction training) and supervision of all staff;

- Ensuring that sufficient staff are employed to enable them to do their jobs properly, for example, for social workers, for all cases to be allocated, without staff workloads being too high;

- Having systems in place to provide information, for example on whether work done is appropriate, effective and in accordance with procedures;

- Providing services out of hours and to cover holidays and sickness absence;

- The organisation of reception systems, including receipt of telephone referrals; and

- The roles and responsibilities of specific professionals, particularly named and designated health professionals and designated persons in schools and further education institutions, including, where appropriate to the role, the provision of dedicated sessions for their safeguarding work.

56. These two core documents will be supplemented by short pieces of guidance on specific client groups or processes, or aimed at particular groups of staff, some of which are already published or in preparation. Nobody will need to use all the pieces of guidance, although everyone will use the core and probably one or two of the supplementaries. This suite of *Children's Services Guidance* will be completed within two years, thus meeting Lord Laming's timescales.

57. The following new, or very recent, guidance will also cover issues raised by the reports:

- Police protection powers, through a new circular, to be issued shortly;

- A revised *Prison Service Order (PSO) 4950 Regimes for Prisoners Under 18 Years Old*, to take full account of the recent judgment, which found that the Children Act 1989 continues to apply to children in prison, subject to the requirements of their imprisonment. Annex B to the PSO outlines a co-operative, multi-agency approach to ensure the welfare of children in Prison Service establishments is safeguarded;

- A recent Local Authority Circular (LAC(2003)13) on homelessness and the use of section 17 of the Children Act 1989, which covers issues about local authority responsibility for children whose families' needs for housing have been met, as in Victoria's case, by the local authority providing them with accommodation outside their area;

- Guidance under section 175 of the Education Act 2002, to assist Local Education Authorities (and the governing bodies of maintained schools and further education institutions) with their duty to make arrangements to ensure that their functions are exercised with a view to safeguarding and promoting the welfare of children. The guidance will clarify LEAs' responsibilities to provide advice and support to maintained schools about child protection, ensure appropriate training is available for staff, and monitor the effectiveness of procedures and training; and

- Overarching, high-level, Government guidance on the current legal framework for the sharing of personal data, which will cover issues of administrative and common law, and the relevant parts of the Data Protection Act 1998 and the Human Rights Act 1998/European Convention on Human Rights.

Bringing information together

58. In addition to staff working in accordance with the same guidance, and to common standards, it is helpful if staff are able to bring together information, both known within an agency, and from several different organisations, to give a complete picture about the child and family.

59. The Green Paper chapter *Early Intervention and Effective Protection* explains how new information sharing systems will be established to enable concerns to be registered at an early stage and flagged up to all workers. The Green Paper also explains, in the chapter *Accountability and Integration – Locally, Regionally and Nationally*, how front-line workers will become more closely integrated through arrangements such as Children's Trusts. This should help to improve discussion about concerns.

60. The social services contribution to this information sharing, the Integrated Children's System, has been developed to enable information gathered from the point of referral to social services and during assessments to be used more effectively in making plans and deciding on what types of services to provide to children and families. It also provides the basis for reviewing whether a child is making progress in important areas of their development, such as health and education.

61. The Integrated Children's System has been designed to enable local organisations to work together better, share information more easily and facilitate referrals between organisations. It will benefit children and families by enabling them to understand what information organisations are asking for and why, and will help them judge whether they are getting the help they need.

Gathering information

62. Each agency should record information about children and families at the point at which they first come into contact with that specific agency, whether that is when they register with a GP or when they approach social services to ask for support.

63. In at least one of the councils that failed Victoria Climbié, the system for receiving referrals from members of the public was ineffective: callers could be passed around the telephone system, with nobody being prepared to take responsibility for the information that was being provided, or referrals could be lost through poor management of paper systems.

64. In recent years, many councils have altered their arrangements for receiving referrals: some have authority-wide call centres, while others have specific points of contact for social services. In order to assess the impact of these different services, a short piece of research has been commissioned to find out about the range of systems that is in use. The research will also look at the role of voluntary organisations and helplines, including ChildLine and the NSPCC's child protection helpline, and will inform further action.

65. In addition, in response to one of Lord Laming's recommendations, the Department of Health has asked the Royal College of General Practitioners to consider, together with other relevant stakeholders including health visitors and school nurses, whether or not it would be feasible to make any changes to the process for GP registration of new child patients, in order to gather information about the child's home, schooling and other 'social' issues.

66. The Green Paper chapter *Early Intervention and Effective Protection* is consulting on the development of a new unified assessment process, using common terminology, and drawing on the existing assessment tools. The process of developing and using a common core assessment framework will have a critical role to play in improving relationships between professionals. In practice, in areas where such a system has been implemented, it reduced the volume of inappropriate referrals and enabled the recipient to respond to them more quickly and appropriately.

Storing information

67. An essential step towards ensuring that information can be brought together within a single agency is to have a single record for each client or patient. This is clearly going to be easier if that record is electronic. Therefore, the Government is working to develop electronic social care and health records, which will be based around the individual.

68. National strategic implementation programmes – *Delivering 21st Century IT: Support for the NHS* and *Information for Social Care* – will take forward major developments in the use of information technology. The Government launched *Defining the Social Care Record* for consultation on 1st July 2003. In addition, work is underway on the Integrated Care Records Service. This aims to:

- Support the individual and the quick, convenient and seamless delivery of services designed around the individual;

- Support staff in the delivery of integrated care and, through effective electronic communications, and better learning and knowledge management, cut the time required to find essential information (such as notes and test results) and make specialist expertise more accessible; and

- Improve management and delivery of services by providing good quality data to support National Service Frameworks, clinical audit, governance and management information.

69. The delivery of the Integrated Care Records Service will provide an environment which will allow the quick and easy sharing of information between the various care delivery areas. It supports NHS organisations in working with social care organisations and, by facilitating their use of the NHS number, it is a major step towards providing a truly seamless service.

70. The Police Information Technology Organisation, through its Central Customer Directorate, is currently analysing and evaluating child protection IT systems in use by police forces in England and Wales. Following this, the organisation will submit options to the Association of Chief Police Officers by December 2003, and a decision will be made as to whether there should be a national police child protection IT system, taking into account the requirements of other organisations, including social services. If a national system is the preferred option, then an outline business case will be prepared.

71. Electronic systems for managing information make it easier to keep and share information. But organisations without electronic systems still need to have effective systems for storing information about children and families, and ensuring that necessary information is shared with those who need to know.

Sharing information

72. Many professionals and other staff struggle to know when to share information about children and families – this was clear from *Safeguarding Children*, as well as anecdotally. That is why there is a section on information sharing in the booklet *What To Do If You're Worried A Child Is Being Abused*. This booklet is the first time that the Government has provided guidance to steer people through the decisions about when to share information, what to share, with whom and why. It emphasises that a failure to provide information that could have prevented a tragedy could expose people to criticism in the same way as an unjustified disclosure of information. The booklet, and this section in particular, has been widely welcomed by people working with children and families.

73. To help people to implement the guidance, the training materials being commissioned alongside the booklet will cover the issue of information sharing, and again, help people to work their way through the necessary decisions.

74. The electronic health and social care records will help practitioners to build up a better picture of a child and family's circumstances, and the booklet *What To Do If You're Worried A Child Is Being Abused* will help them to refer more appropriately. But the Joint Chief Inspectors' report makes clear that there are serious problems with the use of child protection registers, the local authority-held lists of children in ongoing need of safeguarding, which are used by those outside children's social services to find out whether a child is considered to be at continuing risk of significant harm.

75. The Department of Health commissioned a piece of research, in the light of the report, to see what use was made of child protection registers. The research identified some worrying practices, such as:

- Nearly half the custodians of child protection registers reported that staff who were able to make a direct check of the register were liable to experience a false sense of security over a child, as they perceived being on the register as providing protection for the child;

- On the other hand, 30% of custodians reported that other staff seemed to believe that if a child was not on the register, there was no need for concern; and

- 40% of custodians thought that other organisations viewed being on the child protection register as a 'passport to services'.

76. It is therefore clear that, at least in the short term, some training is necessary for staff on the purpose and use of the child protection register. The Government will therefore commission material on this issue, as part of the training resource to accompany the booklet *What To Do If You're Worried A Child Is Being Abused*.

77. In the longer term, as the Integrated Children's System becomes widely used, it will allow staff to identify those children who, for example, have been the subject of enquiries into whether they are at risk of suffering, or have suffered, significant harm, have been the subject of a child protection conference, or are the subject of a child protection plan. The child protection register will therefore become redundant, and can be phased out gradually across the country alongside the introduction of the Integrated Children's System.

Workforce issues

78. A vital ingredient in a successful safeguarding system is the recruitment and retention of adequate numbers of suitably qualified, competent staff. *Safeguarding Children* showed that there are severe difficulties recruiting and retaining staff in many areas.

79. The Green Paper chapter *Workforce Reform* sets out proposals to attract more people into careers working with children and to support and develop the workforce. The proposals aim to address the underlying problems that affect recruitment and retention, to improve both initial training and professional development and to make it easier to move between roles and work across professional boundaries.

Recruitment and retention

80. In most parts of the children and young people's services sector, specialist child protection staff are usually recruited from among existing appropriately qualified staff in the relevant service. Broader recruitment and retention issues are therefore important. Particular efforts are being made in the social care sector, predominantly through the National Social Care Recruitment Campaign, and by providing new grants for human resources development and training. The workforce strategy of the National Service Framework will also address these issues.

81. The first ever national recruitment and retention campaign for social care was launched in October 2001. The campaign consists of national advertising, leaflets, posters, local and national PR activity, a helpline, and a website. The materials produced are available to local employers to support their own recruitment and retention efforts. The campaign was funded initially for £1.5 million.

82. It aims to increase the number of people applying for social work training by 5000 by 2005/06, inform the public about what social workers and social care workers do, and make existing social workers and social care workers realise that their work is valued. In the 18 months after the campaign was launched, there were over 50,000 calls to the helpline and hits on the website. Over the 12 months to October 2002, there was an increase of at least 6.5% in applications for social work training.

83. The Government has established new Specific Grants to councils for human resources development (£9.5 million in 2003/04, planned to increase almost fivefold within three years), and for training (£25 million in 2003/04, planned to increase almost fourfold by 2005/06).

84. The Training Grant is to support the achievement of targets based on all the new National Minimum Standards under the Care Standards Act 2000. The Human Resource Development Strategy Grant will raise the quality of social care human resources management, deal with recruitment and retention problems, and support reforms in service provision, which will be delivered by the development of new types of worker. The Government expects this to lead to more appropriate use of staff, so that highly trained workers are used only where their skills are essential.

85. Building on this work, the Green Paper sets out proposals for increasing recruitment and retention of all those working with children. These include the development of a more coherent approach to pay for those who work with children. This could, for example, involve moving to multi-year pay agreements to recognise and reward the children's practice workforce, to support recruitment and retention, and to underpin the proposed measures to improve skills and effectiveness. There might also be a comprehensive workload survey to look at how to increase the time spent working with children and families, by cutting out unnecessary paperwork, improving support from supervisors and administrators, and better use of information technology, and a recruitment campaign across all those working with children.

Training

86. The Green Paper chapter *Accountability and Integration – Locally, Regionally and Nationally* explains that the statutory responsibilities of all organisations should be clarified and strengthened to encourage them to play a greater role in safeguarding children. The chapter on *Workforce Reform* sets out proposals for national occupational standards across a number of front-line roles, linked to modular qualifications which allow workers to move between jobs more easily, and a common core of training for those who work solely with children and families and those who have wider roles (such as GPs and the police) to help secure a consistent response to children's and families' needs and a better understanding of professional roles.

87. Safeguarding children already features, to a greater or lesser extent, in the initial qualifying training of most workers with children and young people. In the short term, the Government is seeking to influence the filling of gaps in training programmes to ensure that all workers have an appropriate level of training in safeguarding children. For example:

- From September 2003, a new three-year social work degree course will be introduced to replace the two-year diploma in social work. The curriculum for the new degree is based on National Occupational Standards for Social Work, which include units on assessing the needs of individuals and families, assessing and managing risk to individuals and families and reviewing and updating knowledge of legal, policy and procedural frameworks. It also includes working within multi-disciplinary and multi-organisational teams, networks and systems;

- Prior to reviewing the initial training for social workers, the Department of Health was involved in the development of a Post-Qualifying Child Care Award, which was first run in January 2000. Child care social work activity with children, young people and their families at this level is concerned with safeguarding and promoting the welfare of children and young people and promoting their upbringing by their families, wherever possible, and where necessary by the provision of services. The National Occupational Standards, on which the award is based, reflect this. At least 12,000 social workers could undertake this award and of these at least 919 have done so already. A further 958 social workers are considering undertaking the award in 2003/04;

- The Department for Education and Skills, in consultation with the Teacher Training Agency and employers, is considering what child protection training is needed by teachers and staff filling other roles in the education service, although responsibility for training ancillary and support staff rests, in the main, with Local Education Authorities and schools. The Department for Education and Skills is in the process of mapping and reviewing the training about child protection currently provided or planned as part of pre-qualifying training or induction training for different groups, and this review will be completed by October 2003;

- From 2003, child protection will be an explicit part of police probationer training. The National Crime and Operations Faculty within the Central Police Training and Development Authority (Centrex) has also sent out a training package for in-service training and the Home Office will work with police forces to encourage its implementation in all forces;

- A detailed action plan has been developed and agreed by all stakeholders involved in police training to take forward the recommendations from both reports. The standards to which police officers should be trained in child protection have now been set. Centrex will develop an accredited training programme based on these standards, for all police staff involved in child protection issues. This will be implemented by January 2005;

- The Prison Service duty to safeguard and promote welfare includes ensuring that staff working with children and young people know how to recognise and respond to indicators of abuse; the Prison Service does not have specialist child protection staff but works closely with social services, Area Child Protection Committees and police, following Government guidance;

- The Department of Health is supporting work by the Royal College of Paediatrics and Child Health to develop training materials on safeguarding children, through funding a two-year research fellow in association with the Royal College. The research fellow will take forward this work with the NSPCC, with a view to the training materials being available by the end of 2005, for use as a permanent feature in paediatric training programmes;

- The Government is funding the preparation of multi-agency training materials to support the implementation of Government guidance, following the publication of the booklet *What To Do If You're Worried A Child Is Being Abused*, which will help people to work through difficult issues, and consider sensitivities around working with children and families, including around race, culture and language; and

- Work has started to identify the basic skills and competencies needed to deliver quality care for children in special circumstances. A working group has commissioned the development of a framework to describe what people need to know and be able to do. This framework will be completed by the end of 2003, and will contain practical tools for local service and workforce planners to support education commissioning and team development.

88. In addition to this work, the then Secretary of State for Health said, on publication of the report of the Victoria Climbié Inquiry, "The Home Secretary and I also intend to ask the professional bodies responsible for training police, social services and NHS staff in child protection to oversee a review of training needs including inter-agency training".

89. This review, involving all the relevant training bodies in health, social care, education and police, is being conducted in two stages. The initial stage aimed to identify current standards for inter-agency training. It found that, for all of the professions considered, there were very few standards that were directly designed for inter-agency training and working, although there were many more that were relevant. In addition, although mechanisms existed to ensure practitioners undertook training within, and designed for, their own profession, there were far fewer, if any, effective mechanisms to ensure they undertook any inter-agency training.

90. The findings from this first stage will inform the second stage, which will identify, by the end of September 2003, recommendations on what changes need to be implemented to improve inter-agency training, taking account of best practice in inter-agency working. It will then set out a timetable and process for implementation.

Other issues

Public protection issues

91. In order to target offenders, the Government is further developing the Violent and Sex Offender Register and improving the way sex offenders are managed in the community via Multi-Agency Public Protection Arrangements. A taskforce has been established to tackle on-line child abuse and paedophilia and new legislation (some currently before Parliament) should increase the punishment available for sexual offences and sexual exploitation.

92. Multi-Agency Public Protection Arrangements are being strengthened in the Criminal Justice Bill currently before Parliament. The Bill will impose, on all those organisations whose work can contribute to public protection work, including social services, housing authorities and Youth Offending Teams, a 'duty to co-operate' with the police and probation services in each area. The nature of that duty will be formally defined in each area by a memorandum which the Bill will require the parties to draw up.

93. The Government has taken action to address the problems highlighted by *Safeguarding Children* around relationships between Multi-Agency Public Protection Panels and other child protection arrangements, including, in time, Local Safeguarding Children Boards. This will be addressed in implementing the 'duty to co-operate' provisions of the Criminal Justice Bill. The Home Secretary will add a further section to the Multi-Agency Public Protection Arrangements guidance on this aspect of the development of the Multi-Agency Public Protection Arrangements. This addition to the guidance will reflect the emerging developments on the new local structures to support improved child protection. Following its issue and in anticipation of the measures contained in the Criminal Justice Bill, work will begin to embed Multi-Agency Public Protection Arrangements good practice in standards that can be audited.

Private fostering

94. As recommended by Lord Laming, the Government has carried out a review of private fostering, which found that the critical factor in whether or not children in private fostering arrangements are safeguarded is that councils with social services responsibilities take a proactive approach in discharging their existing duties under the Children Act 1989 and the Children (Private Arrangements for Fostering) Regulations 1991. The standards and monitoring of council activity on private fostering will therefore be strengthened.

95. National Minimum Standards for Private Fostering will be introduced, which will be enforced through inspections by the Commission for Social Care Inspection. The National Minimum Standards will require councils to take a more proactive approach to identifying private fostering arrangements. The standards will be issued in 2004.

96. This will be monitored by requiring councils to provide information centrally about the numbers of notifications they have of private fostering arrangements. Councils will start collecting this information from April 2004, subject to the agreement of the Statistics Technical Working Group.

97. Work on setting the National Minimum Standards will begin shortly and the current regulations (the Children (Private Arrangements for Fostering) Regulations 1991) will be reviewed alongside this work.

98. The Immigration Service is committed to improving the spread of best practice by immigration officers in safeguarding vulnerable children who seek to enter the United Kingdom. Social services are informed immediately if an immigration officer has reason to believe a child to be at risk of harm.

99. Following a review of the current systems, the Government is proposing to introduce child-specific interview training for immigration officers. The Immigration Service will work in partnership with social services to ensure better dissemination of information on children seeking to enter the United Kingdom.

The services that failed Victoria Climbié

100. The Home Secretary and the then Secretary of State for Health asked the relevant inspectorates to undertake further monitoring of the local services that failed Victoria Climbié, in order to ensure that they are of a satisfactory standard. Haringey was inspected in March 2003, Brent in May 2003, and Ealing and Enfield in July 2003. Full reports of the inspection findings will be published in due course. The findings will be followed up as necessary in each area to ensure that these local services are satisfactory.

How will the Government know whether the system is improving?

Inspections

101. Clearly, in order to know whether or not children are being adequately safeguarded, a comprehensive programme of inspections of all the relevant organisations is essential. These inspections will consider how well systems keep children and families informed and involved in decisions which affect their lives.

102. The recommendations in both reports show some concern about the inspection of inter-agency and single agency arrangements for safeguarding children, and particularly that joint inspections were not undertaken frequently enough, and did not involve enough inspectorates, to gain a complete picture of children's safeguards across the country.

103. Therefore, the Green Paper sets out proposals for a single, integrated framework for inspections of children's services across an area. This framework will cover the quality of provision, outcomes achieved, management capacity, and value for money of services overall. Each service will be assessed on how well it contributes to children's services overall, as well as how well it meets its own objectives.

104. In addition, and more immediately, on publication of the Victoria Climbié Inquiry Report, the Government asked the Chief Inspectors to consider whether there was a need to supplement the planned programme of inspections in any way. All relevant inspectorates, including the National Care Standards Commission, have reviewed their planned individual and joint inspection activity to take account of the recommendations of *Safeguarding Children* and, where appropriate, the Victoria Climbié Inquiry Report. The Chief Inspectors have met to consider the outcome of these reviews and to plan for the next triennial Joint Chief Inspectors' Children's Safeguards Report, due for publication in late 2005. A Steering Group with representation from all the relevant inspectorates, and chaired by the Acting Chief Social Services Inspector, has been established. The review will utilise the wide range of inspection evidence that will be available, to identify the arrangements to safeguard children in the following categories: those living in the community, those living away from home and those involved in the justice system. It is planned to bring together all the knowledge and evidence on how services respond to these groups of children and then to determine what additional cross-inspectorate work might be needed to identify and track how well services work together in responding to the needs of these children.

105. In terms of the work of specific inspectorates, Her Majesty's Inspectorate of Constabulary's 1999 thematic inspection of police forces on child protection recommended the introduction of "a standards-based service for the investigation of abuse against children". In response to this, the Association of Chief Police Officers has prepared draft standards for child protection policing, which will be completed and circulated by the end of 2003. The inspectorate is in the process of rewriting its general child protection inspection protocol, which will complement the standards-based child protection manual, and will also reflect the findings of the police self-audit. Force inspection protocols will address child protection as a specific issue. The inspectorate has, however, decided that it would not be appropriate to use Basic Command Unit inspections as a means to inspect child protection functions, as the inspection teams do not have the necessary expertise, and the focus of these inspections is on leadership and generic performance, and not specific functions. However, it has been agreed that the inspectorate will carry out a formal re-inspection to review progress on the findings of both the 1999 thematic and the Victoria Climbié Inquiry Report. The timing of this will be considered in the autumn as part of a scheduled review of the inspectorate's business strategy.

106. The Government is bringing legislation to establish a new Commission for Healthcare Audit and Inspection and a new Commission for Social Care Inspection. Both new inspectorates will have a specific duty to be concerned with the need to safeguard and promote the rights and welfare of children when exercising their functions. The new Commissions will bring together the inspection of health and

KEEPING CHILDREN SAFE | 23

social care, improve understanding of the quality of health and social care services for children, and make it easier to improve the standards of these services.

Assessing performance

107. The social services performance assessment regime is designed to monitor how well councils are delivering social services for children and adults, identifying poor performance early. Support is available for councils who do not have the capacity to improve their performance themselves, for example, through Performance Action Teams.

108. The Social Services Inspectorate meets with every council each year to discuss areas of good performance, and areas where performance needs to improve. The inspectorate uses a wide set of evidence to assess a council's performance, from performance indicators, inspections and twice-yearly performance monitoring. From 2002, the inspectorate gave each council a performance rating from zero to three stars. Underlying this were separate judgements about adults' and children's services.

109. Within the star rating system, there are minimum performance levels expected for child protection services. For 2003, this will include a performance indicator on child protection review conferences, and will also use the audit of child protection services mentioned earlier. Where inspectors judge that the audit has revealed that a council's child protection services are only serving some people well or worse, then the overall assessment of children's services will not be higher than serving some people well, with a consequent effect on the maximum star rating that a council can achieve.

110. The star rating also informs the Comprehensive Performance Assessment of all local government services. There are incentives for councils to achieve both a good star and Comprehensive Performance Assessment rating, since better performing councils receive significant freedoms including a lighter touch inspection regime. In this way, there is an incentive for councils to improve services, and more resources are available to inspect and support councils whose performance is less good.

111. The NHS performance ratings system provides a high level overview of NHS organisations' performance across a wide range of measures. The rating awarded is based on the trust's performance against a number of key targets, a wider set of 'Balanced Scorecard' performance indicators and the organisation's assessment conducted by the Commission for Health Improvement, the independent regulator for NHS performance. The ratings are from zero to three stars, depending on the level of performance.

112. The key targets reflect the minimum standards the Government expects all organisations to achieve. These targets draw on the Planning and Priorities Framework issued to the NHS for that year. The key targets are pass/fail indicators and are limited in number (currently a maximum of nine).

113. The 'Balanced Scorecard' indicators are divided into three 'focus areas' (clinical, patient, and capacity and capability) and are chosen to assess the quality of the wider range of NHS functions and services. They often link to the Planning and Priorities Framework but will also include other targets and priorities in the NHS Plan, or in key documents such as National Service Frameworks.

Research

114. In addition to information from inspections, it is also vital to have a planned programme of research, to inform policy development and practice in the field.

115. The Department of Health's Policy Research Programme is already supporting research to aid the implementation and development of National Service Frameworks. There are also a number of ongoing studies on child protection under the Costs and Effectiveness and Quality Protects initiatives.

116. In addition, a research initiative on child abuse and protection is planned, subject to the availability of financial resources and agreement of ministers. This is likely to include work relating to issues such as the recognition of abuse, neglect and emotional abuse, child prostitution and inter-agency working.

Learning lessons from experience

117. Even when all these changes are implemented, it is inevitable that on occasion, children will be injured, or even die, whether through accidents or at the hands of their carers. The lessons from these deaths and injuries must be learnt, in an effort to reduce the number of children suffering in this way. However, there are concerns about the current system for serious case reviews, in particular regional and local variations in practice.

118. The Government is therefore seeking views on a new system, where all unexpected child deaths would be examined by local 'screening groups'. This would include all deaths that occur as a result of accidents, suicides and conditions that would normally be considered treatable in this country, such as pneumonia and gastroenteritis, in case neglect or abuse has played a part. Deaths resulting from diagnosed chronic or acute conditions which can be fatal, such as certain forms of cancer, would be excluded, along with deaths that occur due to a congenital abnormality. These screening groups, which would consist of a number of professionals with appropriate expertise nominated by their organisation and appointed by the Local Safeguarding Children Board, would decide which cases should be subject to a serious case review, and which should receive a smaller scale review, perhaps on a single agency basis, and draw out any public health lessons.

119. Proposals for the local screening groups will be developed in consultation with the National Patient Safety Agency to ensure that they are consistent with and build on the Agency's education, training and development programme for NHS trusts, and, in particular, with its staged roll-out of training in Root Cause Analysis as a systematic and thorough technique for NHS organisations to use in investigating the causes of serious patient safety incidents.

120. Serious case reviews would then be carried out by teams that were independent of any of the local statutory organisations involved in safeguarding children, and were appointed by the Local Safeguarding Children Board. The teams would draw up action plans, whose implementation would be monitored.

121. In addition, the Government will ensure that a national overview is taken, so that serious case reviews are carried out when they should be, and are of good quality. Informed by this work, the Government will continue to publish a biennial overview report on serious case reviews. The overview may also point to the need for public health or child safety campaigns.

Conclusion

122. The Government has started to address historical under-funding in relation to family support and child protection by investing heavily in mainstream services, through recent spending reviews, and by allocating additional resources specifically to supporting families and parents, for example, within the context of the child poverty agenda. The Green Paper explains how support for parents and families will be enhanced further.

123. In the longer term, increased investment in prevention and early intervention should reduce the number of children being harmed. But some serious cases, like Victoria Climbié's, are deliberately concealed, and systematically planned. In the shorter term, therefore, increased investment in prevention and early intervention may uncover unmet needs relating to these more serious cases. But by raising the priority given to safeguarding children within all organisations, by giving a wider range of organisations and professionals greater responsibilities to provide support, and by helping practitioners and their managers to work together better, children should be better safeguarded, and the lessons learnt from Victoria's death.

Recommendations from the Victoria Climbié Inquiry Report

Recommendation	Timescale	Decision	Category of Response/Action
Recommendation 1. With the support of the Prime Minister, a ministerial Children and Families Board should be established at the heart of government. The Board should be chaired by a Minister of Cabinet rank and should have ministerial representation from government departments concerned with the welfare of children and families. (paragraph 17.97)	2 years	Accept in principle	The Government agrees that the focus on children's policy needs to be strengthened at the national level. On 13th June 2003, the Prime Minister announced the appointment of Margaret Hodge as the full time Minister for Children, Young People and Families with the Secretary of State for Education and Skills taking the lead responsibility at Cabinet level (Green Paper chapter *Accountability and Integration – Locally, Regionally and Nationally*).
Recommendation 2. The chief executive of a newly established National Agency for Children and Families will report to the ministerial Children and Families Board. The post of chief executive should incorporate the responsibilities of the post of a Children's Commissioner for England. (paragraph 17.97)	2 years	Accept in principle	The Government agrees that the focus on children's policy needs to be strengthened. Therefore, on 13th June 2003, the Prime Minister announced the appointment of Margaret Hodge as the full time Minister for Children, Young People and Families bringing together the responsibility for children's education and social services into one Government Department, and providing a strong focus for children's policy at the national level. There will be new structures at a local level including Children's Trusts and the creation of the post of Director of Children's Services. The Green Paper also sets out proposals for a Children's Commissioner (Green Paper chapter *Accountability and Integration – Locally, Regionally and Nationally*).

Recommendation	Timescale	Decision	Category of Response/Action
Recommendation 3. The newly established National Agency for Children and Families should have the following responsibilities: • To assess, and advise the ministerial Children and Families Board about, the impact on children and families of proposed changes in policy; • To scrutinise new legislation and guidance issued for this purpose; • To advise on the implementation of the UN Convention on the Rights of the Child; • To advise on setting nationally agreed outcomes for children and how they might best be achieved and monitored; • To ensure that legislation and policy are implemented at a local level and are monitored through its regional office network; • To report annually to Parliament on the quality and effectiveness of services to children and families, in particular on the safety of children. (paragraph 17.97)	2 years	Accept in principle, in part	With the appointment of Margaret Hodge as Minister for Children, Young People and Families the Government has signalled a new strengthened focus for children, and the Green Paper sets out a proposal for clear practice standards for children's services, and proposals for strengthening the inspection framework for children's services. The Government will consider what mechanisms are needed to support the Minister for Children, Young People and Families in discharging her responsibilities, in the light of the new national structures. The Green Paper includes proposals for a Children's Commissioner for England. There is already a requirement on the Government to present an annual report to Parliament on the Children Act 1989 (Green Paper chapter *Accountability and Integration – Locally, Regionally and Nationally*).
Recommendation 4. The National Agency for Children and Families will operate through a regional structure which will ensure that legislation and policy are being implemented at local level, as well as providing central government with up-to-date and reliable information about the quality and effectiveness of local services. (paragraph 17.97)	2 years	Accept in principle	The Government will consider what mechanisms are needed to support the Minister for Children, Young People and Families in discharging her responsibilities, in the light of the new national structures.

Recommendation	Timescale	Decision	Category of Response/Action
Recommendation 5. The National Agency for Children and Families should, at their discretion, conduct serious case reviews (Part 8 reviews) or oversee the process if they decide to delegate this task to other agencies following the death or serious deliberate injury to a child known to the services. This task will be undertaken through the regional offices of the Agency with the authority vested in the National Agency for Children and Families to secure, scrutinise and analyse documents and to interview witnesses. I consider it advisable that these case reviews are published, and that additionally, on an annual basis, a report is produced collating the Part 8 review findings for that year. (paragraph 17.97)	2 years	Accept in principle	The Government accepts that the process for serious case reviews needs to be changed, and is consulting on proposals for a new system. Under this, all unexpected child deaths would be screened by local 'screening groups'. These screening groups would decide which cases should be subject to a serious case review, and which should receive a smaller scale review. In addition, there will be a national overview to ensure serious case reviews are carried out on the right cases, to the correct standards, and a periodic overview report on these reviews will be published (paragraphs 117-121).
Recommendation 6. Each local authority with social services responsibilities must establish a Committee of Members for Children and Families with lay members drawn from the management committees of each of the key services. This Committee must ensure the services to children and families are properly co-ordinated and that the inter-agency dimension of this work is being managed effectively. (paragraph 17.97)	6 months	Accept in principle	The Green Paper sets out proposals for each council with social services responsibilities to have a lead member for children and also a Director of Children's Services (Green Paper chapter *Accountability and Integration – Locally, Regionally and Nationally*). The introduction of Children's Trusts to integrate education, health and social care services will co-ordinate interagency provision of services (paragraphs 37-39).

Recommendation	Timescale	Decision	Category of Response/Action
Recommendation 7. The local authority chief executive should chair a Management Board for Services to Children and Families which will report to the Member Committee referred to above. The Management Board for Services to Children and Families must include senior officers from each of the key agencies. The Management Board must also establish strong links with community-based organisations that make significant contributions to local services for children and families. The Board must ensure staff working in the key agencies are appropriately trained and are able to demonstrate competence in their respective tasks. It will be responsible for the work currently undertaken by the Area Child Protection Committee. (paragraph 17.97)	6 months	Accept in principle	Reformed and strengthened Area Child Protection Committees, to be called Local Safeguarding Children Boards, will be established on a statutory basis, with all the key agencies represented and having a duty to co-operate (paragraph 19).
Recommendation 8. The Management Board for Services to Children and Families must appoint a director responsible for ensuring that inter-agency arrangements are appropriate and effective, and for advising the Management Board for Services to Children and Families on the development of services to meet local need. Furthermore, each Management Board for Services to Children and Families should: • Establish reliable ways of assessing the needs and circumstances of children in their area, with particular reference to the needs of children who may be at risk of deliberate harm; • Identify ways of establishing consultation groups of both children and adult users of services. (paragraph 17.97)	2 years	Accept in principle	The Green Paper sets out proposals for a Director for Children's Services to be appointed by each council. The Green Paper chapter *Accountability and Integration – Locally, Regionally and Nationally* sets out further proposals to integrate education, health and social care through development of Children's Trusts (paragraphs 37-39).
Recommendation 9. The budget contributed by each of the local agencies in support of vulnerable children and families should be identified by the Management Board for Services to Children and Families so that staff and resources can be used in the most flexible and effective way. (paragraph 17.97)	6 months	Accept in principle	The pooling of budgets following the introduction of Children's Trusts will facilitate flexibility of staff and resources in the provision of services covering education, health and social care (paragraphs 37-39).

Recommendation	Timescale	Decision	Category of Response/Action
Recommendation 10. As part of their work, the government inspectorates should inspect both the quality of the services delivered, and also the effectiveness of the inter-agency arrangements for the provision of services to children and families. (paragraph 17.97)	6 months	Accept	The Green Paper proposes a single inspection framework for children's services, which will assess quality and look at the contribution of each organisation to children's services generally (paragraphs 101-106).
Recommendation 11. The Government should review the law regarding the registration of private foster carers. (paragraph 17.97)	2 years	Accept	The Government has carried out a review of private fostering and will establish National Minimum Standards for private fostering (paragraphs 94-97).
Recommendation 12. Front line staff in each of the agencies which regularly come into contact with families with children must ensure that in each new contact, basic information about the child is recorded. This must include the child's name, address, age, the name of the child's primary carer, the child's GP, and the name of the child's school if the child is of school age. Gaps in this information should be passed on to the relevant authority in accordance with local arrangements. (paragraph 17.97)	3 months	Accept	This is included in the checklist of good practice recommendations issued on publication of the report (paragraphs 40-47). This is also covered in the booklet *What To Do If You're Worried A Child Is Being Abused* which sets out what information should be collected about a child at first contact (paragraphs 49-52).

Recommendation	Timescale	Decision	Category of Response/Action
Recommendation 13. The Department of Health should amalgamate the current Working Together and the National Assessment Framework documents into one simplified document. The document should tackle the following six aspects in a clear and practical way: • It must establish a 'common language' for use across all agencies to help those agencies to identify who they are concerned about, why they are concerned, who is best placed to respond to those concerns, and what outcome is being sought from any planned response. • It must disseminate a best practice approach by social services to receiving and managing information about children at the 'front door'. • It must make clear in cases that fall short of an immediately identifiable section 47 label that the seeking or refusal of parental permission must not restrict the initial information gathering and sharing. This should, if necessary, include talking to the child. • It must prescribe a clear step-by-step guide on how to manage a case through either a section 17 or a section 47 track, with built-in systems for case monitoring and review. • It must replace the child protection register with a more effective system. Case conferences should remain, but the focus must no longer be on whether to register or not. Instead, the focus should be on establishing an agreed plan to safeguard and promote the welfare of the particular child. • The new guidance should include some consistency in the application of both section 17 and section 47. (paragraph 17.111)	2 years	Accept	a) The booklet *What To Do If You're Worried A Child Is Being Abused* covers some points (paragraphs 49-52). b) The revision of the Children Act 1989 guidance will include two volumes of core guidance accompanied by additional supplementaries, and this guidance will cover all these points (paragraphs 53-55). c) In the short to medium term, the training materials commissioned to accompany the booklet *What To Do If You're Worried A Child Is Being Abused* will include a section on child protection registers. In the longer term, the Integrated Children's System will eventually make child protection registers unnecessary (paragraph 77).

Recommendation	Timescale	Decision	Category of Response/Action
Recommendation 14. The National Agency for Children and Families should require each of the training bodies covering the services provided by doctors, nurses, teachers, police officers, officers working in housing departments, and social workers to demonstrate that effective joint working between each of the these professional groups features in their national training programmes. (paragraph 17.114)	2 years	Accept in Principle	A review of training is currently being undertaken to be completed by the end of September 2003. The review will examine this issue and make recommendations about future inter-agency training (paragraphs 88-90).
Recommendation 15. The newly created local Management Boards for Services to Children and Families should be required to ensure training on an inter-agency basis is provided. The effectiveness of this should be evaluated by the government inspectorates. Staff working in the relevant agencies should be required to demonstrate that their practice with respect to inter-agency working is up to date by successfully completing appropriate training courses. (paragraph 17.114)	6 months	Accept in Principle	A review of training is currently being undertaken to be completed by the end of September 2003. The review will examine this issue and make recommendations about future inter-agency training (paragraphs 88-90).
Recommendation 16. The Government should issue guidance on the Data Protection Act 1998, the Human Rights Act 1998, and common law rules on confidentiality. The Government should issue guidance as and when these impact on the sharing of information between professional groups in circumstances where there are concerns about the welfare of children and families. (paragraph 17.116)	2 years	Accept	An appendix in the booklet *What To Do If You're Worried A Child Is Being Abused* covers information sharing for practitioners and the Government will shortly issue high level guidance covering issues of administrative and common law, as well as the relevant parts of the Data Protection Act 1998 and the Human Rights Act 1998/European Convention on Human Rights (paragraphs 52, 57 and 72).

Recommendation	Timescale	Decision	Category of Response/Action
Recommendation 17. The Government should actively explore the benefit to children of setting up and operating a national children's database on all children under the age of 16. A feasibility study should be a prelude to a pilot study to explore its usefulness in strengthening the safeguards for children. (paragraph 17.121)	2 years	Accept in principle	Better information sharing is crucial. The booklet *What To Do If You're Worried A Child Is Being Abused* contains an appendix on information sharing (paragraph 52). The Government's Identification, Referral and Tracking Project is exploring how information about children can be shared appropriately within and between agencies, and more easily transferred across local authority boundaries, to make sure children receive the services tailored to their needs at the earliest opportunity (paragraphs 58-61).
Recommendation 18. When communication with a child is necessary for the purposes of safeguarding and promoting that child's welfare, and the first language of that child is not English, an interpreter must be used. In cases where the use of an interpreter is dispensed with, the reasons for so doing must be recorded in the child's notes/case file. (paragraph 6.251)	3 months	Accept	This is included in the checklist of good practice recommendations issued on publication of the report (paragraphs 40-47). This is also covered in the booklet *What To Do If You're Worried A Child Is Being Abused* (paragraphs 49-52).
Recommendation 19. Managers of duty teams must devise and operate a system which enables them immediately to establish how many children have been referred to their team, what action is required to be taken for each child, who is responsible for taking that action, and when that action must be completed. (paragraph 4.14)	3 months	Accept	This is included in the checklist of good practice recommendations issued on publication of the report (paragraphs 40-47).

Recommendation	Timescale	Decision	Category of Response/Action
Recommendation 20. Directors of Social Services must ensure that staff in their children and families' intake teams are experienced in working with children and families, and that they have received appropriate training. (paragraph 4.16)	6 months	Accept	This is included in the checklist of good practice recommendations issued on publication of the report (paragraphs 40-47). The revision of the Children Act 1989 guidance will include two volumes of core guidance accompanied by additional supplementaries. The core guidance to organisations included in this will cover responsibilities for training staff (paragraphs 53-55).
Recommendation 21. When a professional makes a referral to social services concerning the well-being of a child, the fact of that referral must be confirmed in writing by the referrer within 48 hours. (paragraph 4.59)	3 months	Accept	This is included in the checklist of good practice recommendations issued on publication of the report (paragraphs 40-47). Also included in the booklet *What To Do If You're Worried A Child Is Being Abused* (paragraphs 49-52).
Recommendation 22. If social services place a child in temporary accommodation, an assessment must be made of the suitability of that accommodation and the results of that assessment must be recorded on the child's case file. If the accommodation is unsuitable, this should be reported to a senior officer. (paragraph 4.77)	3 months	Accept	This is covered in the Local Authority Circular on homelessness and the use of section 17 of the Children Act 1989 (LAC(2003)13) (paragraph 57).
Recommendation 23. If social services place a child in accommodation in another local authority area, they must notify that local authority's social services department of the placement. Unless specifically agreed in writing at team manager level by both authorities or above, the placing authority must retain responsibility for the child concerned. (paragraph 4.82)	3 months	Accept	This is included in the checklist of good practice recommendations issued on publication of the report (paragraphs 40-47). This is also covered in the Local Authority Circular on homelessness and the use of section 17 of the Children Act 1989 (LAC(2003)13) (paragraph 57).

Recommendation	Timescale	Decision	Category of Response/Action
Recommendation 24. Where, during the course of an assessment, social services establish that a child of school age is not attending school, they must alert the education authorities and satisfy themselves that, in the interim, the child is subject to adequate daycare arrangements. (paragraph 4.143)	3 months	Accept	This is included in the checklist of good practice recommendations issued on publication of the report (paragraphs 40-47). The Green Paper chapter *Accountability and Integration – Locally, Regionally and Nationally* proposes changes to structures at a local level including Children's Trusts which will improve the integration of education and social services.
Recommendation 25. All social services assessments of children and families, and any action plans drawn up as a result, must be approved in writing by a manager. Before giving such approval, the manager must ensure that the child and the child's carer have been seen and spoken to. (paragraph 4.152)	3 months	Accept	This is included in the checklist of good practice recommendations issued on publication of the report (paragraphs 40-47).
Recommendation 26. Directors of social services must ensure that no case involving a vulnerable child is closed until the child and the child's carer have been seen and spoken to, and a plan for the ongoing promotion and safeguarding of the child's welfare has been agreed. (paragraph 4.183)	3 months	Accept	This is included in the checklist of good practice recommendations issued on publication of the report (paragraphs 40-47).
Recommendation 27. Chief executives and lead members of local authorities with social services responsibilities must ensure that children's services are explicitly included in their authority's list of priorities and operational plans. (paragraph 5.4)	6 months	Accept	This is included in the checklist of good practice recommendations issued on publication of the report (paragraphs 40-47). Also covered by Alan Milburn's letter of 28th January 2003 reminding Chief Executives of their responsibilities (paragraph 21).

Recommendation	Timescale	Decision	Category of Response/Action
Recommendation 28. The Department of Health should require chief executives of local authorities with social services responsibilities to prepare a position statement on the true picture of the current strengths and weaknesses of their 'front door' duty systems for children and families. This must be accompanied by an action plan setting out the timescales for remedying any weaknesses identified. (paragraph 5.9)	6 months	Accept	This is included in the checklist of good practice recommendations issued on publication of the report (paragraphs 40-47).
Recommendation 29. Directors of social services must devise and implement a system which provides them with the following information about the work of the duty teams for which they are responsible: • Number of children referred to the teams; • Number of those children who have been assessed as requiring a service; • Number of those children who have been provided with the service that they require; • Number of children referred who have identified needs which have yet to be met. (paragraph 5.24)	6 months	Accept	This is included in the checklist of good practice recommendations issued on publication of the report (paragraphs 40-47).
Recommendation 30. Directors of social services must ensure that senior managers inspect, at least once every three months, a random selection of case files and supervision notes. (paragraph 5.27)	3 months	Accept	This is included in the checklist of good practice recommendations issued on publication of the report (paragraphs 40-47). The revision of the Children Act 1989 guidance will include two volumes of core guidance accompanied by additional supplementaries. The core guidance to organisations included in this will cover managerial and supervisory responsibilities (paragraphs 53-55).

Recommendation	Timescale	Decision	Category of Response/Action
Recommendation 31. Directors of social services must ensure that all staff who work with children have received appropriate vocational training, receive a thorough induction in local procedures and are obliged to participate in regular continuing training so as to ensure that their practice is kept up to date. (paragraph 5.30)	6 months	Accept	This is included in the checklist of good practice recommendations issued on publication of the report (paragraphs 40-47). The Green Paper chapter *Workforce Reform* makes proposals for training and development of all staff working with children and families.
Recommendation 32. Local authority chief executives must ensure that only one electronic database system is used by all those working in children and families' services for the recording of information. This should be the same system in use across the council, or at least compatible with it, so as to facilitate the sharing of information, as appropriate. (paragraph 5.46)	2 years	Accept	The development of a national electronic social care record is a key step in ensuring that only one electronic database system is used. The Government launched *Defining the Electronic Social Care Record* for consultation on 1st July 2003 (paragraph 68).
Recommendation 33. Local authorities with responsibility for safeguarding children should establish and advertise a 24 hour free telephone referral number for use by members of the public who wish to report concerns about a child. A pilot study should be undertaken to evaluate the feasibility of electronically recording calls to such a number. (paragraph 5.71)	2 years	Accept in principle	The Government is commissioning research to see what works best of the variety of systems in place in local authorities to receive referrals (paragraph 64).
Recommendation 34. Social workers must not undertake home visits without being clear about the purpose of the visit, the information to be gathered during the course of it, and the steps to be taken if no one is at home. No visits should be undertaken without the social worker concerned checking the information known about the child by other child protection agencies. All visits must be written up on the case file. (paragraphs 5.108 and 6.606)	6 months	Accept	This is included in the checklist of good practice recommendations issued on publication of the report (paragraphs 40-47).

Recommendation	Timescale	Decision	Category of Response/Action
Recommendation 35. Directors of social services must ensure that children who are the subject of allegations of deliberate harm are seen and spoken to within 24 hours of the allegation being communicated to social services. If this timescale is not met, the reason for the failure must be recorded on the case file. (paragraph 5.127)	3 months	Accept in principle	The booklet *What To Do If You're Worried A Child Is Being Abused* advises that social workers must see the child 'within a timescale that is appropriate to the nature of the concerns expressed at referral'. It is not always in the best interests of the child to see them immediately, for example, where it may endanger the child (paragraphs 49-52).
Recommendation 36. No emergency action on a case concerning an allegation of deliberate harm to a child should be taken without first obtaining legal advice. Local authorities must ensure that such legal advice is available 24 hours a day. (paragraph 5.128)	3 months	Accept	The booklet *What To Do If You're Worried A Child Is Being Abused* makes clear that legal advice should always be sought when time allows (paragraphs 49-52).
Recommendation 37. The training of social workers must equip them with the confidence to question the opinion of professionals in other agencies when conducting their own assessment of the needs of the child. (paragraph 5.138)	6 months	Accept in principle	This is included in the checklist of good practice recommendations issued on publication of the report (paragraphs 40-47). The Royal College of Paediatrics and Child Health is working with the Government to identify the key issues around differences of opinion between staff within and between agencies, and decide how to take these forward, probably as part of the revisions to the Children Act 1989 guidance or through training (paragraphs 34-36). The Green Paper chapter *Workforce Reform* makes proposals for training and development of all staff working with children and families.
Recommendation 38. Directors of social services must ensure that the transfer of responsibility of a case between local authority social services departments is always recorded on the case file of each authority, and is confirmed in writing by the authority to which responsibility for the case has been transferred. (paragraph 5.152)	3 months	Accept	This is included in the checklist of good practice recommendations issued on publication of the report (paragraphs 40-47).

Recommendation	Timescale	Decision	Category of Response/Action
Recommendation 39. All front line staff within local authorities must be trained to pass all calls about the safety of children through to the appropriate duty team without delay, having first recorded the name of the child, his or her address, and the nature of the concern. If the call cannot be put through immediately, further details from the referrer must be sought (including their name, address and contact number). The information must then be passed verbally and in writing to the duty team within the hour. (paragraph 5.169)	3 months	Accept	This is included in the checklist of good practice recommendations issued on publication of the report (paragraphs 40-47).
Recommendation 40. Directors of social services must ensure that no case that has been opened in response to allegations of deliberate harm to a child is closed until the following steps have been taken: • The child has been spoken to alone. • The child's carers have been seen and spoken to. • The accommodation in which the child is to live has been visited. • The views of all the professionals involved have been sought and considered. • A plan for the promotion and safeguarding of the child's welfare has been agreed. (paragraph 5.187)	3 months	Accept	The booklet *What To Do If You're Worried A Child Is Being Abused* sets out the process to be used when making enquiries about a child who may be at risk of or who has suffered significant harm (paragraphs 49-52).
Recommendation 41. Chief executives of local authorities with social services responsibilities must make arrangements for senior managers and councillors to regularly visit intake teams in their children's services department, and to report their findings to the chief executive and social services committee. (paragraph 5.193)	6 months	Accept	This is included in the self audit tool that followed the checklist of good practice recommendations issued on publication of the report (paragraphs 40-47).

Recommendation	Timescale	Decision	Category of Response/Action
Recommendation 42. Directors of social services must ensure that where the procedures of a social services department stipulate requirements for the transfer of a case between teams within the department, systems are in place to detect when such a transfer does not take place as required. (paragraph 6.7)	3 months	Accept	This is included in the checklist of good practice recommendations issued on publication of the report (paragraphs 40-47). The revision of the Children Act 1989 guidance will include two volumes of core guidance accompanied by additional supplementaries. The core guidance to organisations included in this will cover management information systems (paragraphs 53-55).
Recommendation 43. No social worker should undertake section 47 inquiries unless he or she has been trained to do so. Directors of social services must undertake an audit of staff currently carrying out section 47 inquiries to identify gaps in training and experience. These must be addressed immediately. (paragraph 6.12)	6 months	Accept	This is included in the checklist of good practice recommendations issued on publication of the report (paragraphs 40-47). The revision of the Children Act 1989 guidance will include two volumes of core guidance accompanied by additional supplementaries. The core guidance to organisations included in this will outline the responsibilities for ensuring staff are adequately trained (paragraphs 53-55).
Recommendation 44. When staff are temporarily promoted to fill vacancies, directors of social services must subject such arrangements to six-monthly reviews and record the outcome. (paragraph 6.29)	3 months	Accept	This is included in the checklist of good practice recommendations issued on publication of the report (paragraphs 40-47). The revision of the Children Act 1989 guidance will include two volumes of core guidance accompanied by additional supplementaries. The core guidance to organisations included in this will outline the responsibilities for ensuring staff are adequately trained (paragraphs 53-55).

Recommendation	Timescale	Decision	Category of Response/Action
Recommendation 45. Directors of social services must ensure that the work of staff working directly with children is regularly supervised. This must include the supervisor reading, reviewing and signing the case file at regular intervals. (paragraph 6.59)	3 months	Accept	This is included in the checklist of good practice recommendations issued on publication of the report (paragraphs 40-47). The revision of the Children Act 1989 guidance will include two volumes of core guidance accompanied by additional supplementaries. The core guidance to organisations included in this will cover the responsibilities for ensuring staff are adequately trained and supervised (paragraphs 53-55).
Recommendation 46. Directors of social services must ensure that the roles and responsibilities of child protection advisers (and those employed in similar posts) are clearly understood by all those working within children's services. (paragraph 6.71)	3 months	Accept	This is included in the checklist of good practice recommendations issued on publication of the report (paragraphs 40-47).
Recommendation 47. The chief executive of each local authority with social services responsibilities must ensure that specialist services are available to respond to the needs of children and families 24 hours a day, seven days a week. The safeguarding of children should not be part of the responsibilities of general out-of-office-hours teams. (paragraph 6.181)	2 years	Accept in principle	The revision of the Children Act 1989 guidance will include two volumes of core guidance accompanied by additional supplementaries. The core guidance to organisations included in this will cover out of hours services (paragraphs 53-55).
Recommendation 48. Directors of social services must ensure that when children and families are referred to other agencies for additional services, that referral is only made with the agreement of the allocated social worker and/or their manager. The purpose of the referral must be recorded contemporaneously on the case file. (paragraph 6.263)	3 months	Accept in principle	The booklet *What To Do If You're Worried A Child Is Being Abused* covers referrals making clear that it is important to make sure, however, that planned referrals are not delayed by sick or annual leave (paragraphs 49-52).

Recommendation	Timescale	Decision	Category of Response/Action
Recommendation 49. When a professional from another agency expresses concern to social services about their handling of a particular case, the file must be read and reviewed, the professional concerned must be met and spoken to, and the outcome of this discussion must be recorded on the case file. (paragraph 6.289)	3 months	Accept	This is included in the checklist of good practice recommendations issued on publication of the report (paragraphs 40-47).
Recommendation 50. Directors of social services must ensure that when staff are absent from work, systems are in place to ensure that post, e-mails and telephone contacts are checked and actioned as necessary. (paragraph 6.318)	3 months	Accept	This is included in the checklist of good practice recommendations issued on publication of the report (paragraphs 40-47).
Recommendation 51. Directors of social services must ensure that all strategy meetings and discussions involve the following three basic steps: • A list of action points must be drawn up, each with an agreed timescale and the identity of the person responsible for carrying it out. • A clear record of the discussion or meeting must be circulated to all those present and all those with responsibility for an action point. • A mechanism for reviewing completion of the agreed actions must be specified. The date upon which the first such review is to take place is to be agreed and documented. (paragraph 6.575)	3 months	Accept	This is included in the checklist of good practice recommendations issued on publication of the report (paragraphs 40-47).

Recommendation	Timescale	Decision	Category of Response/Action
Recommendation 52. Directors of social services must ensure that no case is allocated to a social worker unless and until his or her manager ensures that he or she has the necessary training, experience and time to deal with it properly. (paragraph 6.581)	6 months	Accept	This is included in the checklist of good practice recommendations issued on publication of the report (paragraphs 40-47). The revision of the Children Act 1989 guidance will include two volumes of core guidance accompanied by additional supplementaries. The core guidance to organisations included in this will outline responsibilities for ensuring staff are adequately trained (paragraphs 53-55).
Recommendation 53. When allocating a case to a social worker, the manager must ensure that the social worker is clear as to what has been allocated, what action is required and how that action will be reviewed and supervised. (paragraph 6.586)	3 months	Accept	This is included in the checklist of good practice recommendations issued on publication of the report (paragraphs 40-47).
Recommendation 54. Directors of social services must ensure that all cases of children assessed as needing a service have an allocated social worker. In cases where this proves to be impossible, arrangements must be made to maintain contact with the child. The number, nature and reasons for such unallocated cases must be reported to the social services committee on a monthly basis. (paragraph 6.589)	6 months	Accept	This is included in the checklist of good practice recommendations issued on publication of the report (paragraphs 40-47). The revision of the Children Act 1989 guidance will include two volumes of core guidance accompanied by additional supplementaries. The core guidance to organisations included in this will outline responsibilities for ensuring adequate staffing. This recommendation is not an acceptable substitute for adequate staffing, but can be an emergency stopgap (paragraphs 53-55).
Recommendation 55. Directors of social services must ensure that only those cases in which a social worker is actively engaged in work with a child and the child's family are deemed to be 'allocated'. (paragraph 6.590)	3 months	Accept	This is included in the checklist of good practice recommendations issued on publication of the report (paragraphs 40-47).

Recommendation	Timescale	Decision	Category of Response/Action
Recommendation 56. Directors of social services must ensure that no child known to social services who is an inpatient in a hospital and about whom there are child protection concerns is allowed to be taken home until it has been established by social services that the home environment is safe, the concerns of the medical staff have been fully addressed, and there is a social work plan in place for the ongoing promotion and safeguarding of that child's welfare. (paragraph 6.594)	3 months	Accept	This is included in the checklist of good practice recommendations issued on publication of the report (paragraphs 40-47). The revision of the Children Act 1989 guidance will include two volumes of core guidance accompanied by additional supplementaries. The core guidance to organisations included in this will discuss inter-agency working (paragraphs 53-55).
Recommendation 57. Directors of social services must ensure that social work staff are made aware of how to access effectively information concerning vulnerable children which may be held in other countries. (paragraph 6.619)	6 months	Accept	This is included in the checklist of good practice recommendations issued on publication of the report (paragraphs 40-47). The booklet *What To Do If You're Worried A Child Is Being Abused* also covers this in detail (paragraphs 49-52).
Recommendation 58. Directors of social services must ensure that every child's case file includes, on the inside of the front cover, a properly maintained chronology. (paragraph 6.629)	6 months	Accept	This is included in the checklist of good practice recommendations issued on publication of the report (paragraphs 40-47). The booklet *What To Do If You're Worried A Child Is Being Abused* also covers this (paragraphs 49-52).
Recommendation 59. Directors of social services must ensure that staff working with vulnerable children and families are provided with up-to-date procedures, protocols and guidance. Such practice guidance must be located in a single-source document. The work should be monitored so as to ensure procedures are followed. (paragraph 8.7)	6 months	Accept	The booklet *What To Do If You're Worried A Child Is Being Abused* provides procedures for all staff (paragraphs 49-52).
Recommendation 60. Directors of social services must ensure that hospital social workers working with children and families are line managed by the children and families' section of their social services department. (paragraph 8.19)	6 months	Accept	This is included in the self audit tool that followed up the checklist of good practice recommendations issued on publication of the report (paragraphs 40-47).

Recommendation	Timescale	Decision	Category of Response/Action
Recommendation 61. Directors of social services must ensure that hospital social workers participate in all hospital meetings concerned with the safeguarding of children. (paragraph 8.27)	3 months	Accept	This is included in the checklist of good practice recommendations issued on publication of the report (paragraphs 40-47).
Recommendation 62. Where hospital-based social work staff come into contact with children from other local authority areas, the directors of social services of their employing authorities must ensure that they work to a single set of guidance agreed by all the authorities concerned. (paragraph 8.53)	6 months	Accept	The booklet *What To Do If You're Worried A Child Is Being Abused* is this single set of guidance (paragraphs 49-52).
Recommendation 63. Hospital social workers must always respond promptly to any referral of suspected deliberate harm to a child. They must see and talk to the child, to the child's carer and to those responsible for the care of the child in hospital, while avoiding the risk of appearing to coach the child. (paragraph 8.100)	3 months	Accept	This is included in the checklist of good practice recommendations issued on publication of the report (paragraphs 40-47). Also covered by the booklet *What To Do If You're Worried A Child Is Being Abused* (paragraphs 49-52).
Recommendation 64. When a child is admitted to hospital and deliberate harm is suspected, the nursing care plan must take full account of this diagnosis. (paragraph 9.35)	3 months	Accept	This is included in the checklist of good practice recommendations issued on publication of the report (paragraphs 40-47).
Recommendation 65. When the deliberate harm of a child is identified as a possibility, the examining doctor should consider whether taking a history directly from the child is in that child's best interests. When that is so, the history should be taken even when the consent of the carer has not been obtained, with the reason for dispensing with consent recorded by the examining doctor. *Working Together* guidance should be amended accordingly. In those cases in which English is not the first language of the child concerned, the use of an interpreter should be considered. (paragraph 9.39)	6 months	Accept	An appendix on data sharing is included in *What To Do If You're Worried A Child Is Being Abused* covering the areas of consent and confidentiality. The booklet also covers communicating with a child (paragraphs 49-52).

Recommendation	Timescale	Decision	Category of Response/Action
Recommendation 66. When a child has been examined by a doctor, and concerns about deliberate harm have been raised, no subsequent appraisal of these concerns should be considered complete until each of the concerns has been fully addressed, accounted for and documented. (paragraph 9.60)	3 months	Accept	This is included in the checklist of good practice recommendations issued on publication of the report (paragraphs 40-47).
Recommendation 67. When differences of medical opinion occur in relation to the diagnosis of possible deliberate harm to a child, a recorded discussion must take place between the persons holding the different views. When the deliberate harm of a child has been raised as an alternative diagnosis to a purely medical one, the diagnosis of deliberate harm must not be rejected without full discussion and, if necessary, obtaining a further opinion. (paragraph 9.65)	6 months	Accept	This is included in the checklist of good practice recommendations issued on publication of the report (paragraphs 40-47). The Royal College of Paediatrics and Child Health is working with the Government to identify the key issues around differences of opinion between staff within and between agencies, and decide how to take these forward, probably as part of the revisions to the Children Act 1989 guidance or through training (paragraphs 34-36).
Recommendation 68. When concerns about the deliberate harm of a child have been raised, doctors must ensure that comprehensive and contemporaneous notes are made of these concerns. If doctors are unable to make their own notes, they must be clear about what it is they wish to have recorded on their behalf. (paragraphs 9.72 and 10.30)	3 months	Accept	This is included in the checklist of good practice recommendations issued on publication of the report (paragraphs 40-47). The booklet *What To Do If You're Worried A Child Is Being Abused* also covers the issue of record keeping (paragraphs 49-52).
Recommendation 69. When concerns about the deliberate harm of a child have been raised, a record must be kept in the case notes of all discussions about the child, including telephone conversations. When doctors and nurses are working in circumstances in which case notes are not available to them, a record of all discussions must be entered in the case notes at the earliest opportunity so that this becomes part of the child's permanent health record. (paragraph 9.95)	3 months	Accept	This is included in the checklist of good practice recommendations issued on publication of the report (paragraphs 40-47). The booklet *What To Do If You're Worried A Child Is Being Abused* also covers the issue of record keeping (paragraphs 49-52).

Recommendation	Timescale	Decision	Category of Response/Action
Recommendation 70. Hospital trust chief executives must introduce systems to ensure that no child about whom there are child protection concerns is discharged from hospital without the permission of either the consultant in charge of the child's care or of a paediatrician above the grade of senior house officer. Hospital chief executives must introduce systems to monitor compliance with this recommendation. (paragraphs 9.101 and 10.145)	6 months	Accept	This is included in the checklist of good practice recommendations issued on publication of the report (paragraphs 40-47). The revision of the Children Act 1989 guidance will include two volumes of core guidance accompanied by additional supplementaries. The core guidance to organisations included in this will cover safe transfer from hospital to community in the context of interagency work (paragraphs 53-55).
Recommendation 71. Hospital chief executives must introduce systems to ensure that no child about whom there are child protection concerns is discharged from hospital without a documented plan for the future care of the child. The plan must include follow up arrangements. Hospital chief executives must introduce systems to monitor compliance with this recommendation. (paragraphs 9.101 and 10.146)	6 months	Accept	This is included in the checklist of good practice recommendations issued on publication of the report (paragraphs 40-47). The revision of the Children Act 1989 guidance will include two volumes of core guidance accompanied by additional supplementaries. The core guidance to organisations included in this will cover safe transfer from hospital to community in the context of interagency work (paragraphs 53-55).
Recommendation 72. No child about whom there are concerns about deliberate harm should be discharged from hospital back into the community without an identified GP. Responsibility for ensuring this happens rests with the hospital consultant under whose care the child has been admitted. (paragraph 9.105)	3 months	Reject	It cannot be the responsibility of the hospital consultant to force anyone to register with a GP. However, the revision of the Children Act 1989 guidance will include two volumes of core guidance accompanied by additional supplementaries. The core guidance to organisations included in this will cover safe transfer from hospital to community in the context of interagency working and follow up (paragraphs 53-55).

Recommendation	Timescale	Decision	Category of Response/Action
Recommendation 73. When a child is admitted to hospital and deliberate harm is suspected, the doctor or nurse admitting the child must inquire about previous admissions to hospital. In the event of a positive response, information concerning the previous admissions must be obtained from the other hospitals. The consultant in charge of the case must review this information when making decisions about the child's future care and management. Hospital chief executives must introduce systems to ensure compliance with this recommendation. (paragraph 10.36)	6 months	Accept	This is included in the checklist of good practice recommendations issued on publication of the report (paragraphs 40-47).
Recommendation 74. Any child admitted to hospital about whom there are concerns about deliberate harm must receive a full and fully-documented physical examination within 24 hours of their admission, except when doing so would, in the opinion of the examining doctor, compromise the child's care or the child's physical and emotional well-being. (paragraph 10.41)	3 months	Accept	This is included in the checklist of good practice recommendations issued on publication of the report (paragraphs 40-47).
Recommendation 75. In a case of possible deliberate harm to a child in hospital, when permission is required from the child's carer for the investigation of such possible deliberate harm, or for the treatment of the child's injuries, the permission must be sought by a doctor above the grade of senior house officer. (paragraph 10.73)	3 months	Accept	This is included in the checklist of good practice recommendations issued on publication of the report (paragraphs 40-47).
Recommendation 76. When a child is admitted to hospital with concerns about deliberate harm, a clear decision must be taken as to which consultant is to be responsible for the child protection aspects of the child's care. The identity of that consultant must be clearly marked in the child's notes so that all those involved in the child's care are left in no doubt as to who is responsible for the case. (paragraph 10.105)	3 months	Accept	This is included in the checklist of good practice recommendations issued on publication of the report (paragraphs 40-47). The booklet *What To Do If You're Worried A Child Is Being Abused* makes clear that a child's notes should identify a relevant lead in each agency (paragraphs 49-52).

Recommendation	Timescale	Decision	Category of Response/Action
Recommendation 77. All doctors involved in the care of a child about whom there are concerns about possible deliberate harm must provide social services with a written statement of the nature and extent of their concerns. If misunderstandings of medical diagnosis occur, these must be corrected at the earliest opportunity in writing. It is the responsibility of the doctor to ensure that his or her concerns are properly understood. (paragraph 10.162)	3 months	Accept	This is included in the checklist of good practice recommendations issued on publication of the report (paragraphs 40-47).
Recommendation 78. Within a given location, health professionals should work from a single set of records for each child. (paragraph 11.39)	3 months	Accept	An electronic patient record system is in progress, but it is not due for implementation before 2008 (paragraphs 67-69). In the meantime, the booklet *What To Do If You're Worried A Child Is Being Abused* emphasises the importance of accurate, full and contemporaneous record keeping (paragraphs 49-52).
Recommendation 79. During the course of a ward round, when assessing a child about whom there are concerns about deliberate harm, the doctor conducting the ward round should ensure that all available information is reviewed and taken account of before decisions on the future management of the child's case are taken. (paragraph 11.39)	3 months	Accept	This is included in the checklist of good practice recommendations issued on publication of the report (paragraphs 40-47).
Recommendation 80. When a child for whom there are concerns about deliberate harm is admitted to hospital, a record must be made in the hospital notes of all face-to-face discussions (including medical and nursing 'handover') and telephone conversations relating to the care of the child, and of all decisions made during such conversations. In addition, a record must be made of who is responsible for carrying out any actions agreed during such conversations. (paragraph 11.39)	3 months	Accept	This is included in the checklist of good practice recommendations issued on publication of the report (paragraphs 40-47). The booklet *What To Do If You're Worried A Child Is Being Abused* emphasises the importance of good record keeping (paragraphs 49-52).

Recommendation	Timescale	Decision	Category of Response/Action
Recommendation 81. Hospital chief executives must introduce systems to ensure that actions agreed in relation to the care of a child about whom there are concerns of deliberate harm are recorded, carried through and checked for completion. (paragraph 11.39)	6 months	Accept	This is included in the checklist of good practice recommendations issued on publication of the report (paragraphs 40–47).
Recommendation 82. The Department of Health should examine the feasibility of bringing the care of children about whom there are concerns about deliberate harm within the framework of clinical governance. (paragraph 11.39)	6 months	Accept	The hospital standard of the National Service Framework for Children, Young People and Maternity Services addresses care of children about whom there are concerns of abuse or neglect (paragraph 31).
Recommendation 83. The investigation and management of a case of possible deliberate harm to a child must be approached in the same systematic and rigorous manner as would be appropriate to the investigation and management of any other potentially fatal disease. (paragraph 11.53)	6 months	Accept	The hospital standard of the National Service Framework for Children, Young People and Maternity Services addresses the investigation and management of a case of possible abuse or neglect (paragraph 31).
Recommendation 84. All designated and named doctors in child protection and all consultant paediatricians must be revalidated in the diagnosis and treatment of deliberate harm and in the multi-disciplinary aspects of a child protection investigation. (paragraph 11.53)	2 years	Accept	Annual appraisal is being introduced for all NHS staff. New licences to practise for doctors, revalidated periodically, are being issued by the General Medical Council. The data from annual appraisal will inform the revalidation process (paragraph 33).
Recommendation 85. The Department of Health should invite the Royal College of Paediatrics and Child Health to develop models of continuing education in the diagnosis and treatment of the deliberate harm of children, and in the multi-disciplinary aspects of a child protection investigation, to support the revalidation of doctors described in the preceding recommendation. (paragraph 11.53)	2 years	Accept	The Department of Health is supporting work by the Royal College of Paediatrics and Child Health to develop training materials on child protection through funding a two-year research fellow in association with the College. The College will take forward this work with the NSPCC, with a view to the training materials being available by the end of 2005 (paragraph 87).

Recommendation	Timescale	Decision	Category of Response/Action
Recommendation 86. The Department of Health should invite the Royal College of General Practitioners to explore the feasibility of extending the process of new child patient registration to include gathering information on wider social and developmental issues likely to affect the welfare of the child, for example their living conditions and their school attendance. (paragraph 12.29)	2 years	Accept in principle	The Royal College of General Practitioners has been invited to hold a workshop to explore how to take this forward (paragraph 65) and has indicated that it will be doing so.
Recommendation 87. The Department of Health should seek to ensure that all GPs receive training in the recognition of deliberate harm to children, and in the multi-disciplinary aspects of a child protection investigation, as part of their initial vocational training in general practice, and at regular intervals of no less than three years thereafter. (paragraph 12.29)	2 years	Accept	The Government is funding the preparation of multi-agency training materials to support the implementation of Government guidance, following the publication of the booklet *What To Do If You're Worried A Child Is Being Abused* (paragraph 87).
Recommendation 88. The Department of Health should examine the feasibility of introducing training in the recognition of deliberate harm to children as part of the professional education of all general practice staff and for all those working in primary healthcare services for whom contact with children is a regular feature of their work. (paragraph 12.29)	2 years	Accept	The Government is funding the preparation of multi-agency training materials to support the implementation of Government guidance, following the publication of the booklet *What To Do If You're Worried A Child Is Being Abused* (paragraph 87).
Recommendation 89. All GPs must devise and maintain procedures to ensure that they, and all members of their practice staff, are aware of whom to contact in the local health agencies, social services and the police in the event of child protection concerns in relation to any of their patients. (paragraph 12.29)	6 months	Accept	This is included in the checklist of good practice recommendations issued on publication of the report (paragraphs 40-47). The circular covering the booklet *What To Do If You're Worried A Child Is Being Abused* asked Chief Executives to add contact details before distributing to staff.

Recommendation	Timescale	Decision	Category of Response/Action
Recommendation 90. Liaison between hospitals and community health services plays an important part in protecting children from deliberate harm. The Department of Health must ensure that those working in such liaison roles receive child protection training. Compliance with child protection policies and procedures must be subject to regular audit by primary care trusts. (paragraph 12.57)	6 months	Accept	The Government is funding the preparation of multi-agency training materials to support the implementation of Government guidance, following the publication of the booklet *What To Do If You're Worried A Child Is Being Abused* (paragraph 87). A revision of the Children Act 1989 guidance will include two volumes of core guidance accompanied by additional supplementaries. The core guidance to organisations will cover safe transfer from hospital to community in the context of interagency working and follow up (paragraphs 53-55).
Recommendation 91. Save in exceptional circumstances, no child is to be taken into police protection until he or she has been seen and an assessment of his or her circumstances has been undertaken. (paragraph 13.17)	3 months	Accept	This is included in the checklist of good practice recommendations issued on publication of the report (paragraphs 40-47). A police protection powers circular due to be issued shortly will include this (paragraph 57).
Recommendation 92. Chief constables must ensure that crimes involving a child victim are dealt with promptly and efficiently, and to the same standard as equivalent crimes against adults. (paragraph 13.24)	3 months	Accept	This is included in the checklist of good practice recommendations issued on publication of the report (paragraphs 40-47).
Recommendation 93. Whenever a joint investigation by police and social services is required into possible injury or harm to a child, a manager from each agency should always be involved at the referral stage, and in any further strategy discussion. (paragraph 13.52)	3 months	Accept	The booklet *What To Do If You're Worried A Child Is Being Abused* suggests that 'you and your manager should discuss' to encourage early and continuing involvement of managers (paragraphs 49-52).
Recommendation 94. In cases of serious crime against children, supervisory officers must, from the beginning, take an active role in ensuring that a proper investigation is carried out. (paragraph 13.55)	3 months	Accept	This is included in the checklist of good practice recommendations issued on publication of the report (paragraphs 40-47). Also covered in the booklet *What To Do If You're Worried A Child Is Being Abused* (paragraphs 49-52).

Recommendation	Timescale	Decision	Category of Response/Action
Recommendation 95. The Association of Chief Police Officers must produce and implement the standards-based service, as recommended by Her Majesty's Inspectorate of Constabulary in the 1999 thematic inspection report, *Child Protection*. (paragraph 13.66)	2 years	Accept	ACPO has prepared draft standards for child protection policing. These will be produced by the National Centre of Policing Excellence (NCPE) by the end of 2003 as part of a manual of guidance (paragraph 105).
Recommendation 96. Police forces must review their systems for taking children into police protection and ensure they comply with the Children Act 1989 and Home Office guidelines. In particular, they must ensure that an independent officer of at least inspector rank acts as the designated officer in all cases. (paragraph 13.68)	6 months	Accept	A police protection powers circular due to be issued shortly will include this (paragraph 57). Also, this is included in the checklist of good practice recommendations issued on publication of the report (paragraphs 40-47).
Recommendation 97. Chief constables must ensure that the investigation of crime against children is as important as the investigation of any other form of serious crime. Any suggestion that child protection policing is of a lower status than other forms of policing must be eradicated. (paragraph 14.15)	6 months	Accept	This is included in the checklist of good practice recommendations issued on publication of the report (paragraphs 40-47).
Recommendation 98. The guideline set out at paragraph 5.8 of *Working Together* must be strictly adhered to: whenever social services receive a referral which may constitute a criminal offence against a child, they must inform the police at the earliest opportunity. (paragraph 14.46)	3 months	Accept	This is included in the checklist of good practice recommendations issued on publication of the report (paragraphs 40-47). Also covered in the booklet *What To Do If You're Worried A Child Is Being Abused* (paragraphs 49-52).
Recommendation 99. The *Working Together* arrangements must be amended to ensure the police carry out completely, and exclusively, any criminal investigation elements in a case of suspected injury or harm to a child, including the evidential interview with a child victim. This will remove any confusion about which agency takes the 'lead' or is responsible for certain actions. (paragraph 14.57)	2 years	Accept in principle	The revision of the Children Act 1989 guidance will include two volumes of core guidance accompanied by additional supplementaries. The core guidance to organisations will cover organisational responsibility but interviewing must be consistent with the Government guidance, *Achieving Best Evidence* (paragraphs 53-55).

Recommendation	Timescale	Decision	Category of Response/Action
Recommendation 100. Training for child protection officers must equip them with the confidence to question the views of professionals in other agencies, including doctors, no matter how eminent those professionals appear to be. (paragraph 14.73)	2 years	Accept in principle	The Royal College of Paediatrics and Child Health is working with the Government to identify the key issues around differences of opinion between staff within and between agencies, and decide how to take these forward, probably as part of the revisions to the Children Act 1989 guidance or through training (paragraphs 34-36).
Recommendation 101. The Home Office, through her Majesty's Inspectorate of Constabulary, must take a more active role in maintaining high standards of child protection investigation by means of its regular Basic Commands Unit and force inspections. In addition, a follow-up to the Child Protection thematic inspection of 1999 should be conducted. (paragraph 14.132)	2 years	Accept in part	The police inspectorate has decided that it would not be appropriate to incorporate child protection into Basic Command Unit inspections because the inspection teams lack the necessary expertise, and because the focus of these inspections is on leadership and generic performance, and not specific functions. The inspectorate has decided to carry out a formal re-inspection to review progress on the findings of both the 1999 thematic inspection and the Victoria Climbié Inquiry Report (paragraph 105).
Recommendation 102. The Home Office, through Centrex and the Association of Chief Police Officers, must devise and implement a national training curriculum for child protection officers as recommended in 1999 by Her Majesty's Inspectorate of Constabulary in its thematic inspection report, *Child Protection*. (paragraph 15.16)	2 years	Accept	A detailed action plan has been developed and agreed by all stakeholders to take forward recommendations relating to police training (paragraph 87).

Recommendation	Timescale	Decision	Category of Response/Action
Recommendation 103. Chief constables must ensure that officers working on child protection teams are sufficiently well trained in criminal investigation, and that there is always a substantial core of fully trained detective officers on each team to deal with the most serious inquiries. (paragraph 15.24)	2 years	Accept	A police working group has agreed that child protection teams should be staffed by trained detectives by the end of 2005 (paragraph 24).
Recommendation 104. The Police Information Technology Organisation (PITO) should evaluate the child protection IT systems currently available, and make recommendations to chief constables, who must ensure that their police force has in use an effective child-protection database and IT management system. (paragraph 15.40)	2 years	Accept	The Police Information Technology Organisation (PITO) is analysing and evaluating child protection IT systems used by police forces and will make recommendations to Chief Constables by the end of 2003 (paragraph 70).
Recommendation 105. Chief constables must ensure that child protection teams are fully integrated into the structure of their forces and not disadvantaged in terms of accommodation, equipment or resources. (paragraph 15.45)	6 months	Accept	The police force responses to the checklist provided to the Home Office have given the Government a detailed picture of the current status of child protection teams across forces and will help the Government decide what action to take to ensure that child protection is given the status it needs within forces, and the resource implications (paragraphs 40-47).
Recommendation 106. The Home Office must ensure that child protection policing is included in the list of ministerial priorities for the police. (paragraph 15.46)	6 months	Accept	The National Policing Plan, published in November 2002, sets out the Government's priorities for the police. Child protection was specifically included in these priorities (paragraph 22).
Recommendation 107. Chief constables and police authorities must give child protection investigations a high priority in their policing plans, thereby ensuring consistently high standards of service by well-resourced, well-managed and well-motivated teams. (paragraph 15.46)	6 months	Accept	The National Policing Plan, published in November 2002, sets out the Government's priorities for the police. For the first time, child protection was specifically included in these priorities. Local plans received by the Home Office in March 2003 are consistent with this (paragraphs 22-23).

Recommendation	Timescale	Decision	Category of Response/Action
Recommendation 108. The Home Office, through Centrex, must add specific training relating to child protection policing to the syllabus for the strategic command course. This will ensure that all future chief officers in the police service have adequate knowledge and understanding of the roles of child protection teams. (paragraph 15.53)	6 months	Accept	Training for the strategic command course is currently under review (paragraph 87).

Recommendations from the Joint Chief Inspectors' Report *Safeguarding Children*

Recommendation	Timescale	Decision	Category of Response/Action
Recommendation 2.1 DH, HO, DfES and LCD should ensure the safeguarding of children is firmly and consistently reflected in national and local service planning.		Accept	The Green Paper stresses that the Government will raise the priority given to safeguarding children and each Department has taken some action e.g. including child protection in the National Policing Plan (paragraphs 18-25).
Recommendation 2.2 DH, HO, DfES and LCD should support and facilitate national and local agencies to recruit and retain sufficient levels of appropriately qualified staff, paying particular regard to the image, status, morale, remuneration and working conditions of specialist child protection staff.		Accept	The Green Paper chapter *Workforce Reform* includes proposals for all staff working with children. The Government is also supporting and encouraging work to recruit individual professional groups (paragraphs 80-85).
Recommendation 2.3 DH, HO, DfES and LCD should establish minimum expectations, standards and curriculum for child protection training as part of the core professional training of all professionals working with children and young people (e.g. teacher training, medical and health staff training, police training, etc).		Accept	The Green Paper sets out proposals for a common core of training for all those working with children and families. Each Department is also supporting and encouraging work on individual professional groups (paragraphs 86-87).
Recommendation 2.4 DH should review the current arrangements for Area Child Protection Committees (ACPCs) to determine whether they should be established on a statutory basis to ensure adequate accountability, authority and funding.		Accept	Reformed and strengthened Area Child Protection Committees, to be called Local Safeguarding Children Boards, will be established on a statutory basis, with all the key agencies represented and having a duty to co-operate (paragraph 19).
Recommendation 2.5 DH should review the purpose of child protection registers and issue guidance to local authorities.		Accept	In the short to medium term, the training materials commissioned to accompany the booklet *What To Do If You're Worried A Child Is Being Abused* will include a section on the purpose and use of child protection registers. In the longer term, the Integrated Children's System will eventually make child protection registers unnecessary (paragraphs 74-77).

Recommendation	Timescale	Decision	Category of Response/Action
Recommendation 2.6 LCD, HO and DH should ensure that there is clear guidance provided to all agencies under their respective responsibilities on the implications of the Data Protection Act 1998 and the Human Rights Act 1998 and other relevant law, in respect of sharing information about children where there are welfare concerns.		Accept	An appendix in the booklet *What To Do If You're Worried A Child Is Being Abused* covers information sharing for practitioners and the Government will shortly issue high level guidance covering issues of administrative and common law, as well as the relevant parts of the Data Protection Act 1998 and the Human Rights Act 1998/European Convention on Human Rights (paragraphs 52, 57 and 72).
Recommendation 2.7 DH and HO, with the YJB should issue immediate guidance to ensure that local Youth Offending Teams (YOTs) and the Crown Prosecution Service (CPS) are invited to become full members of all ACPCs		Accept	YOTs and CPS will be involved in new Local Safeguarding Children Boards (paragraph 19).
Recommendation 2.8 HO and YJB should issue revised guidance to the prison service and the ACPC member organisations on the requirements and arrangements to safeguard children in prisons and Young Offender Institutions (YOIs).		Accept	A revised *Prison Service Order 4950 Regimes for Prisoners Under 18 Years Old* will be issued. A revision of the Children Act 1989 guidance will include two volumes of core guidance accompanied by additional supplementaries. The core guidance to organisations will cover responsibilities towards children in prisons and YOIs (paragraph 57).
Recommendation 2.9 HO should ensure that safeguarding children and young people is a national priority for police services and the National Probation Service as part of their public protection arrangements, and ensure that this priority is reflected in local service plans.		Accept	The National Policing Plan, published in November 2002, sets out the Government's priorities for the police, and includes child protection. Local plans reflect this. Child protection is also a specific priority for the Probation Service (paragraphs 22-23 and 25).
Recommendation 2.10 HO should review the current arrangements for Multi-Agency Public Protection Panels (MAPPPs) to identify whether they should be established on a statutory basis to ensure adequate accountability, authority, funding and consistency of practice.		Accept	Multi-Agency Public Protection Panels are being strengthened in the Criminal Justice Bill currently before Parliament (paragraphs 92 and 93).

Recommendation	Timescale	Decision	Category of Response/Action
Recommendation 2.11 HO should ensure that the relationship between MAPPPs and ACPCs is clarified.		Accept	The relationship between Multi-Agency Public Protection Panels and other child protection arrangements will be addressed in the implementation of the Criminal Justice Bill currently before Parliament (paragraphs 92 and 93).
Recommendation 2.12 HO should implement a national policy framework for public protection, including MAPPPs and wider children's safeguarding issues, as a matter of priority in order to develop a more consistent approach to the assessment and management of potentially dangerous people.		Accept in principle	New arrangements as set out in the Criminal Justice Bill will provide a consistent approach to managing potentially dangerous people (paragraphs 91-93).
Recommendation 2.13 HO should issue a set of national standards and performance measures for police and probation services' joint management of potentially dangerous offenders.		Accept in principle	New arrangements as set out in the Criminal Justice Bill will provide a consistent approach to managing potentially dangerous people (paragraphs 91-93).
Recommendation 2.14 All relevant inspectorates should review their inspection activity to ensure that there is sufficient emphasis on examining arrangements to safeguard children.		Accept	A review of inspection activity is underway (paragraph 104). The Green Paper chapter Accountability and Integration – Locally, Regionally and Nationally proposes the creation of a single inspection framework for children's services.

Recommendation	Timescale	Decision	Category of Response/Action
Recommendation 2.15 All relevant inspectorates should ensure that prior to the next report appropriate inspection activity has been undertaken on the following safeguarding areas: Young offender institutions; Residential independent schools; The impact of domestic violence on children; Children looked after outside of their home authority; Unaccompanied asylum-seeking children and the children of refugees and asylum seekers; Children with disabilities; The work of YOTs; Children living in all forms of residential care.		Accept	A review of inspection activity is underway to ensure that all necessary and appropriate inspection activity is undertaken (paragraph 104).
Recommendation 2.16 All relevant inspectorates should ensure that the findings of the National Care Standards Commission in relation to arrangements for safeguarding children in residential and boarding schools and residential care for children and young people are included in future joint Chief Inspectors' reports.		Accept	The National Care Standards Commission is involved in the review of inspection activity that is underway (paragraph 104).
Recommendation 2.17 ACPCs with their constituent agencies should develop integrated planning processes in partnership with MAPPPs to ensure that the safeguarding of children is an individual agency and inter-agency priority.		Accept in principle	Reformed and strengthened Area Child Protection Committees, to be called Local Safeguarding Children Boards, will be required to work with MAPPPs (paragraph 93).
Recommendation 2.18 ACPCs with their constituent agencies should review their constitution, membership, level of representation and funding arrangements to ensure that the committee is adequately resourced and fit for purpose to lead the children's safeguarding agenda across the area and in all relevant settings.		Accept in principle	Reformed and strengthened Area Child Protection Committees, to be called Local Safeguarding Children Boards, will be established on a statutory basis, with all the key agencies represented and having a duty to co-operate (paragraph 19).

Recommendation	Timescale	Decision	Category of Response/Action
Recommendation 2.19 ACPCs with their constituent agencies should ensure that there is an appropriate range and quantity of joint and single agency training to meet the needs of the workforce of constituent agencies (including non-specialist staff), relevant voluntary and independent organisations in their locality, and agree minimum expectations in terms of attendance and content of training.		Accept in principle	A review of training is currently being undertaken. The review is considering the training of all staff and is to be completed by the end of September 2003 (paragraphs 88-90). The Green Paper chapter *Workforce Reform* makes proposals for a common core of training for those who work with children and families.
Recommendation 2.20 ACPCs with their constituent agencies should ensure that there are robust management information processes to support the monitoring, evaluation and auditing of local child protection procedures and practice.		Accept in principle	The revision of the Children Act 1989 guidance will include two volumes of core guidance accompanied by additional supplementaries. The core guidance to organisations will cover management information systems (paragraphs 53-55).
Recommendation 2.21 ACPCs with their constituent agencies should ensure that reviews of serious cases are undertaken on all appropriate cases within the timescales and expectations of Chapter 8 of Working Together to Safeguard Children, that reports are circulated appropriately and action plan recommendations are implemented.		Reject	The Government agrees that the process for serious case reviews needs to be changed, and is consulting on proposals for a new system. Under this, all unexpected child deaths would be screened by local 'screening groups'. These screening groups would decide which cases should be subject to a serious case review, and which should receive a smaller scale review. In addition, there will be a national overview to ensure serious case reviews are carried out on the right cases, to the correct standards, and a periodic overview report on these reviews will be published (paragraphs 117-121).
Recommendation 2.22 ACPCs with their constituent agencies should develop explicit arrangements for sharing information within a framework of joint protocols in order to strengthen the safeguarding of children.		Accept in principle	The booklet *What To Do If You're Worried A Child Is Being Abused* sets out guidance on information sharing (paragraphs 49-52).

Recommendation	Timescale	Decision	Category of Response/Action
Recommendation 2.23 ACPCs with their constituent agencies should ensure that concerns about the safety of young offenders are identified and addressed in partnership with the local YOT, YOIs and prisons.		Accept in principle	Reformed and strengthened Area Child Protection Committees, to be called Local Safeguarding Children Boards, will address concerns about the safety of young offenders (paragraph 19).
Recommendation 2.24 ACPCs with their constituent agencies should review the local arrangements for maintaining and accessing the child protection register to ensure that relevant information is captured and used to maximise the safeguarding of children.		Accept in principle	In the short to medium term, the training materials commissioned to accompany the booklet *What To Do If You're Worried A Child Is Being Abused* will include a section on the purpose and use of child protection registers. In the longer term, the Integrated Children's System will eventually make child protection registers unnecessary (paragraphs 74-77).
Recommendation 2.25 SSDs should review the thresholds for providing services, instigating child protection inquiries and convening initial child protection conferences in order to ensure that children are protected from harm, and ensure that there is a shared understanding of these thresholds across all local agencies.		Accept	The revision of the Children Act 1989 guidance will include two volumes of core guidance accompanied by additional supplementaries. The core guidance to organisations will cover these issues (paragraphs 53-55).
Recommendation 2.26 Police services should review and clarify the role, remit, location and status of force child protection units to ensure that all abuse of children is dealt with to a consistently high standard.		Accept	The returns from the checklist of good practice recommendations will give a picture of services across the country and further action will be taken if necessary (paragraphs 40-47).
Recommendation 2.27 Health services should ensure that pre- and post-recruitment checks are undertaken for all appropriate people working with children in the NHS.		Accept	Pre- and post-recruitment checks are already a requirement. However, the revision of the Children Act 1989 guidance will include two volumes of core guidance accompanied by additional supplementaries. The core guidance to organisations will emphasise the importance of these checks (paragraphs 53-55).

Recommendation	Timescale	Decision	Category of Response/Action
Recommendation 2.28 Health services should ensure that workforce plans adequately reflect the workload of child and adolescent mental health services and community paediatric services.		Accept in principle	Locally Workforce Development Confederations develop plans to meet identified workforce pressures. Nationally the Children's Care Group Workforce Team takes a lead in identifying and addressing workforce issues relating to children's services.
Recommendation 2.29 Health services should establish clear lines of responsibility to ensure that there is: Appropriate provision of and support for designated and named doctors and nurses; Appropriate senior representation on ACPCs; The active involvement in and contribution of Primary Care Trusts (PCTs), including GPs, in the local arrangements to safeguard children. Attendance by general and other medical practitioners at initial child protection conferences or the advance provision of written reports; Adequate provision of specialist nurses and doctors to provide services to children looked after.		Accept	The revision of the Children Act 1989 guidance will include two volumes of core guidance accompanied by additional supplementaries. The core guidance to organisations will cover all of these points (paragraphs 53-55).
Recommendation 2.30 LEAs should monitor the efficiency of arrangements in maintained schools to safeguard children, including the effectiveness of child protection procedures and training.		Accept	Guidance will be issued under section 175 of the Education Act 2002 to assist Local Education Authorities with their duty to make arrangements to ensure that functions are exercised with a view to safeguarding and promoting the welfare of children (paragraph 57).

Printed in the UK for The Stationery Office Limited on behalf of the Controller of Her Majesty's Stationery Office

ID 147033 09/03 077240